HELP
from
BEYOND

HELP
from
BEYOND

by

HENRY L. STERN

WALKER AND COMPANY • NEW YORK

First published in the United States of America in 1974 by the Walker Publishing Company, Inc.

Published simultaneously in Canada by Fitzhenry & Whiteside, Limited, Toronto.

ISBN: 0-8027-0444-1

Library of Congress Catalog Card Number: 73-90380

Printed in the United States of America.

Designed by Stephen O. Saxe

10 9 8 7 6 5 4 3 2 1

THIS BOOK is dedicated to my teachers
and guides in spirit who have tendered me
so much so lovingly over the past forty-four years,
and also to my loving wife for her help
and devotion over the past forty-nine years.

ACKNOWLEDGMENTS

NO BOOK of this nature can be brought forth without the help of sources other than the writer's own mind. Ecclesiastes says, "There is nothing new under the sun." And one cannot help but conclude that almost everything we read or hear has been said before, perhaps in different words.

Some of the authors from whom I have benefited are mentioned in these pages. I do want to acknowledge the great significance and value of their works. Other material has derived from actual experiences in the spirit realm and from teachings received from my spiritual mentors.

I also want to thank Hugh C. Sherwood, the well-known journalist, for editing and revising this book and for rendering other substantial help in its preparation and publication.

Many thanks also go to my secretary, Kathryn F. Beloin, who, through the years, has patiently typed and retyped my manuscript and made valid suggestions along the line.

CONTENTS

INTRODUCTION

SPIRITUALISM or spiritism is defined in the dictionary as the belief that spirits of the dead can communicate with the living, especially through persons called mediums.

Is this belief a theory, a science, a creed or an hallucination? Is it based on actual fact or is it the imagining of the credulous or self-deluded?

The question has been written upon, both in fiction and serious studies. The Bible makes mention of the phenomenon as far back as King Saul. Many among us have had some experience, real or imaginary, with apparitions or voices.

Mediums and pseudo-mediums have sprung up in practically every city, town and hamlet. For a consideration, they invite the public to attend sittings or seances. They say they can contact someone beloved yet departed and receive messages and guidance for the living.

Societies for psychical research have been established, both in this country and abroad, for the purpose of studying and investigating various phenomena, either physical or intangible, and journals are published to discuss and clarify the questions these phenomena raise.

Library shelves contain many volumes dealing with the question, written by people well known in the ranks of science and by others not so noted. On the other hand, there are books labeling the theory a delusion and its adherents culpable hare-brains.

Of late, experiments have been conducted at some of our universities, dealing with extrasensory perception and possible continuation of human intelligence and consciousness after death.

What is the average human being to believe or accept? Nothing but what our senses perceive? Or all reports on the existence of psychic phenomena? Where is the line of demarcation? What are we to accept, what shall we reject?

Deep religious conviction has brought to many a sense of contact with the "supernatural," as evidenced by the numerous reports of departed saints seen by children and attested to by grownups. The miracles at Lourdes and other places are noteworthy examples.

Many reports forecasting future events have been skeptically heard, only to be proved accurate thereafter.

Most religions forbid spiritualistic contact or practice. Both the Old and New Testaments place strict injunction against it, thereby affirming rather than denying the possibility of contacting or communicating with the dead. We are taught that, upon death, the body is returned to the dust and the spirit returns to God. Try as you will to have this further explained by your priest, minister or rabbi, you will probably learn nothing.

We are told about some mysterious hereafter for which we must prepare—of heaven, hell and purgatory, of fires that scorch and burn the sinner who has not repented. But all of it sounds vague, uncertain and unconvincing.

What are we to believe or accept? Where are we to begin

and, having begun, where will it lead us? Will our quest lead to tranquility and perhaps teach us to come nearer to our Maker? Or will it throw us into a state of confusion and further disbelief? Will the thought of some departed loved one, hovering about us in spirit, tend to upset us and disturb our privacy? Or is the grave the end of all?

Just as one man's meat may be the other fellow's poison, so can these questions and the answers thereto be a boon or a curse. In some instances, they may bring light and comfort; in others, a disturbing element that can and has upset people to such a degree that even their sanity has been affected.

In writing this chronicle I want to tell of my own experiences with spiritualism and speak simply, so that I may reach all levels. If I begin to ramble and theorize from time to time, I hope the reader will forgive me since, at this stage, it has become a philosophy, a tenet, a part of my very life.

I do not advise everyone to try spiritual communication, since to many it has proved upsetting. Still I hope that this book will yield an insight into what I believe to be the universal truth, and bring solace to the bereaved and light to the seeker after truth.

My tale may be homiletic. It is not intended to be. If you glean a few crumbs of truth herein, my purpose will have been achieved. In accepting it I have found peace and light. It is my purpose to share that with God's children.

Let there be light.

Chapter 1

Death in
the Family

MY TALE begins in the year 1930. I was then, as now, in the public accounting profession. In my capacity as auditor and business advisor to many firms, I had always been accustomed to view everything from the mathematical or business standpoint, to weigh and balance factors, and to translate everything into dollars and cents.

In my profession, there is no room for "ifs," "ands" or "buts," no room for conjecture. The practical view must be taken and accuracy used and followed at all times.

I was thirty years old in 1930 and had been reared in an Orthodox Jewish home where religious custom was not observed too strictly. I had attended synagogue irregularly, and after twelve years' contact with the New York business world was prone to be cynical.

Competition in general, the elbowing and pushing in particular, the dog-eat-dog attitude in those lean days, did not tend to soften one toward his fellow man or to create a spiritualistic attitude toward life. Cynicism ruled the roost and hardened the heart. You struck the first blow and pushed harder than the next fellow. It was the law of self-preservation.

An event took place, at the beginning of that year, that wrought a great change in me. My brother Sam's eight-year-old child was killed by a truck. We had all loved him and called him by the pet name Bubbie. The death of the child nearly broke his parents' hearts. Anything we said, in our weak attempt at consolation, seemed wasted.

Some months after, I heard from another member of my family that my brother had been searching out various mediums in an effort to contact his son. All of us began to worry about it, and I was delegated to talk to him and to convince him that he was riding for a bad fall and, at best, would be fleeced by a bunch of leeches who purported to be mediums or fortunetellers.

At the time, I must have forgotten a very vivid experience my family once shared with this brother. We were living in Brzezany, state of Galicia, Austria-Hungary, and around 1905, when my brother was about ten years old, a wagon driver nicknamed Chuneh Bazdigah was kicked by his horse in a vital spot and pronounced dead. The accident took place on a Friday morning. In accordance with Jewish Orthodox laws, the body had to be buried before sunset and before the beginning of the Sabbath.

Two nights later, my brother had a very vivid dream in which the dead man appeared before him and complained that he was choking. The following night the same dream took place again. Why the dead man should have appeared to a young boy whom he had hardly known is a mystery.

Upon being told of the dream my father took my brother to the town's rabbi, a learned gentleman renowned far and wide. Convinced that some wrong had been committed, the rabbi obtained authorization to open the grave. In those days, Orthodox Jews, upon death, were wrapped in linen shrouds and laid in the grave, carefully and respectfully, always face up.

When this poor man's grave was opened, he was found dead. The body was twisted sideways and downward, evidence that the man had been buried alive. He might have been in a coma after he was kicked and, in those days of limited knowledge and lack of physicians, it is easily conceivable that folks acted too hurriedly.

There were other instances in which my brother said he had seen ghosts or apparitions, but these incidents came back to my mind only later.

Following the death of my nephew, however, I met my brother and made the most of my plea, telling him that if he persisted in going along in this manner, I feared for his sanity, since it was obvious that it had become an obsession with him.

Sam listened to my harangue for a long while, then asked me if I had learned during my schooling to investigate matters before I condemned. I answered in the affirmative. He then asked that I read a book or two on spiritualism. I refused, saying all I knew was that two and two make four and that I was not interested in old women's tales. I was quite vehement in my argument and much surprised at his calmness.

My brother then told me that he had learned table-tipping, a crude and elementary method of communicating with the departed through a system of signals. He asked me if I would join him in a table-tipping seance. Here was my chance to show him how wrong he was, to really demonstrate to him how far afield he had gone. So I decided to play along and to hoist him by his own petard.

He also invited me to accompany him to the residence of a well-known medium, Frank Decker, in New York the following Thursday night. Again, I accepted.

We then placed a small end table between us and, facing each other, put the palms of our hands flat upon the table top. After a few minutes, I felt a throbbing motion under my palms and the table began to tip first toward my brother, then toward me.

Through the prearranged code, as my brother explained to me, the unseen operator announced himself as Bubbie and tried to show his happiness at my being there by constantly moving the table toward me. We asked him a number of questions which he answered by "yes" or "no"—one tip or two tips. A great pity welled in me for my brother. Had his sorrow brought him to such a low mental point?

But when I thought it was time for me to clear the air of this nonsense, I asked Bubbie if he knew where his father and I planned to go the following Thursday night. "Yes" came the reply.

Since both my parents were still in this life, I asked him if he had seen my departed grandfather. Again, he replied, "Yes." Could he transmit a message to my grandfather? "Yes." Then I requested that my grandfather speak to me on Thursday, and Bubbie promised to mention it.

By that time I was on the verge of cancelling everything, but I felt I might hurt my brother by doing so and might best accomplish my plan by going along. Upon inquiry, my brother told me that he had never visited Frank Decker before and that the arrangement had been made by a third party, whom I was to meet at Decker's.

By Thursday I had arranged to bring along two mutual friends who I thought would help me persuade my brother of the error of his way. When Thursday night came, there were four of us from our neighborhood in addition to another group who had come for similar purposes. All told, there were about twenty-five people at the seance, mostly strangers to each other.

After all lights had been dimmed, everyone was asked to join in singing hymns, which they did. I asked my brother where Frank Decker sat and received a reply from Decker himself that he was right near me. I kept speaking with him sotto voce, from time to time.

After a few minutes of singing, a voice came from almost nowhere, greeting all present and telling us that he was the medium's control and would try to contact each sitter's loved ones "across the veil," so that each might receive a message.

Then a metal trumpet, embellished with a luminous band, began to fly around the room until it stopped before one of the sitters. A voice came through the trumpet identifying the speaker and addressing the sitter. It so continued for a time when, lo and behold, the trumpet stopped before me and a message was delivered to me purporting to come from my grandfather. I was flabbergasted, not so much by its content, which conveyed little that was specific, but by the occurrence itself. My friends and neighbors each received messages from some departed relative, each of whom was identified.

It is easy to see that we three conspirators found ourselves stymied. Instead of condemning my brother, we found our interest aroused.

That evening, after the seance, I met a medium with whom my brother had been sitting for development. Her name was Louisa Riemvis. She had attended the seance with her husband and one of her pupils. We sojourned to a restaurant for refreshment and discussed the Decker seance in detail. Everyone had been impressed—I to the point where I had decided to read a book or two on the subject.

Mrs. Riemvis asked me if I would be interested in attending one of her own seances and I readily accepted. That was the beginning of my experience with spiritualism. As I look back now, it is with a sense of nostalgia. Like kindergarten or freshman year in college, it unfolded for me a new page, a new life.

Chapter 2

Kindergarten of the Soul

THE RIEMVIS family was not wealthy. Fred Riemvis was a printer working for a retail store chain, earning barely enough to maintain his family. His residence was a five-room flat in the Bay Ridge section of Brooklyn, furnished in accordance with his station.

The Riemvises had lost a young son some years previously and, like my brother, found consolation in attending spiritualistic seances. Louisa Riemvis also sat for development and had studied until she became ordained as a minister of the Spiritualist Church, a matter of eight to ten years' time.

She was a woman of large proportion, a lady in every respect and a very gracious person. Utterly sincere and a good Christian, she became a staunch exponent of spiritualism and began to teach and develop others. This was partly for the fees, which were entirely voluntary but which augmented the family's limited income, but mostly in order to give of herself.

Fred Riemvis was also a staunch believer and had become a trance medium, through whom and with whom the spirits did

6

their work. He was—if I may use the expression—an average citizen, good at heart, simple and plain. He might have had as much as a secondary school education, but his general mien and vocabulary made one doubt it.

The class Mrs. Riemvis conducted consisted of five ladies and three men. They met one evening each week. For about thirty minutes a general discussion was held concerning some phase of spiritualism.

After discussion the lights were put out and the seance began with the Lord's Prayer and hymns. It was explained to me that the reason for the prayer was to put each person's mind on a loftier plane and "nearer to God." The purpose of the hymns was to bring all into a relaxed state and harmonious serenity.

I was told that, just as this group was organized of people living on earth, another group was formed on the spirit plane, both meeting for a common purpose. The joint groups working together operated under the name "White Center."

At my first session we sang several hymns. Then Fred Riemvis started to sink into a trance, and it was apparent that someone or something began to use his vocal cords, judging by the various gasps and sounds emanating from him.

A voice came through using Fred's vocal cords, but it was much deeper than his usual tone. The speaker identified himself as Dr. Blake and proceeded first to greet all present and then to deliver a well-worded lecture on spirits and communication. The voice was genteel and well modulated, and the vocabulary and sentence construction bespoke a man highly educated and well-bred. The lecture was lofty.

It was followed by some physical manifestations of spirit power, such as a flying trumpet, a tambourine floating through the air with accompanying sound, and numerous other objects. These were allegedly operated by various Indian spirit guides, including such noted names as Sitting Bull and Red Cloud.

A number of other spirits spoke to us, using either Fred Riemvis' vocal cords or the trumpet, depending—as was explained to me—on their ability and experience. No spirit was allowed to use a trance medium's faculties unless he had previously learned to enter and leave the medium without harming or injuring him.

The spirits conversed with their friends or loved ones at the seance, answering the questions put to them to the best of their ability. Their address and conversation were both light and serious, but all of the spirits conveyed the thought that they were alive, well and "in the light," meaning that they had come into the sphere of light and happy well-being.

One lecture was directed at me. I was told that the record of my life was known to the spirit world and that, although it was their wish that I interest myself in the science of spiritualism, the final choice would be mine and that I would find the answer by myself. The course of my life was mine to choose.

The impression I received during the hour and one-half that the seance lasted was sharp. I heard and witnessed things that were totally new to me. The entire procedure was almost holy. I felt at peace and at rest. It seemed to me that here might be answers to the many questions that arose in my life, answers that I had been unable to glean from either the Bible or from religious services I had attended. I felt as if I were emerging from woods into sunlight.

I learned that in order to hold a seance it was necessary not only to have a competent medium, but also sitters who were quiet, rational people. A nervous or psychotic person or one too fervent in his belief tended to disturb the decorum.

It was also necessary that the spirits be well organized. That meant a high spirit had to be in charge, with deputy spirits controlling various phases and, what was of utmost importance, numerous guarding spirits had to surround the entire procedure and stop any interference from earthbound spirits or poltergeists. The latter might not only disturb the seance, upset the decorum and vitiate the spiritual context, but also attack or attach themselves to the living persons, to their utter detriment. Stories of haunted or obsessed people are abundant.

Generally, throughout the United States, Indian spirits play a great part in spiritualistic circles. The Indians practiced this science during their life on earth and were adept in its manifestations.

Having decided to investigate the matter further, I found a number of books at the New York Public Library. I began with Sir Arthur Conan Doyle and Sir Richard Crookes. Both of them had written about their experiences and were thoroughly convinced and convincing. After reading these authors, I read Sir Oliver Lodge, William James, Emanuel Swedenborg and Frederic Myers.

I returned to the following week's seance, still investigating —thoroughly interested, if not thoroughly convinced. Thinking I had nothing to lose, I joined the developing class.

All the other sitters had become interested for some personal reason. Most had lost someone through death and sought consolation through communication with them.

Such reason was not mine. I was thirty years old, married and had a young son. My financial position was not too secure. The year 1930 followed the financial crash of 1929 and I was caught, with so many others, in a web of economic problems, including job instability and great concern for the future.

Like the man who was all dressed up with no place to go, there I was, educated and well trained, taking odd jobs and earning barely enough to furnish my little family with mere subsistence. I sought an answer, a solution, but found myself up against a stone wall. It seemed hopeless.

At my second sitting, I was told that my problem was known and I was given assurance that, as long as I clung to spiritualism, my livelihood would be assured. I must confess that I

doubted the truth of this, but felt that I should develop whatever ability or aptitude I might have.

And so my schooling began and my interest was aroused. A
sense of curiosity, perhaps even a challenge, opened a new
path and I embarked on it.

Chapter 3

Light on a
Dark Subway

SOMETIME thereafter I began to feel the "call." It is a signal that some spirit wishes to communicate. In my case it was a tightening of the scalp, making me feel as if a tight band had been placed around my head, from the top of my forehead to the base of my skull in the back. The first time I felt this sensation I was riding the subway.

I was seated in a small compartment that was sometimes used by motormen. It gave me a feeling of considerable privacy.

I felt that tight band and I was at a loss as to what to do. I prayed for guidance and, as I shut my eyes, I began to see a number of objects. Naturally I was amazed. It was my first experience with clairvoyance. To the uninitiated, I wish to explain that clairvoyance involves use of the spiritual rather than the physical eyes. As I later learned, these are located just above the eyebrows. The seeing is as actual as if one's physical eyes were used; however, in later stages of development, especially when in a room from which all light is excluded, the

11

same things can be seen with the eyes either open or shut.

As I began to see the various objects, I made it a point to remember them and, when they ceased to appear, I took pencil and paper and jotted them down. Here is what I wrote:

The head of a mule

A human head

An Indian with a blanket of light wrapped around him

An Arab, on horseback, in full native costume

An Indian on horseback, naked to the waist, his face lifted to the sun

Two clouds meeting—one dark, the other light, the lighter boring deeply into the darker and dissipating it.

At home, the same evening, I took my notes and began thinking about them. They were symbolic, I was sure, but what did they mean? I sought help, but it seemed that the matter was left to me to interpret logically. My interpretation was as follows:

Some people will receive all attempts at being told the truth or shown the light in a way comparable to the braying mule. They will swing their heads from side to side, enjoy a hearty guffaw and leave it at that.

Their heads are filled with mundane, everyday thoughts and, although light may shine all about them, it cannot reach inside.

Rather than endeavor to impart knowledge to such people against their will, it is far better to wrap yourself in the light that surrounds you, so that it may keep you spiritually warm and contented.

While an Arab will clothe himself manifold and cover his head, trying to keep the hot sun from him as much as possible, the Indian gladly faces the sun and exposes his body to it. One man's knowledge may be the next fellow's delusion; one man's feast, the next man's poison.

Light and darkness often meet in conflict, but, given time and propelled by God's wisdom, light will bore through and dispel all shadows.

I wrote the above interpretation and brought it with me to class. It was pronounced correct.

At this seance, an Indian named Rainbow announced himself to me. He said he would be my guide and be at my beck and call. He has been with me through the years, a welcome addition to my family and a staunch and abiding friend.

Chapter 4

Three Calls in the Night

SOMETIME after the incident in the subway, I was sitting one evening in my club chair reading a magazine, when I again felt a tight band around my head, signifying that someone wished to speak with me. I laid down the magazine and asked the caller to identify himself. Instead of doing so, he asked me to pick up my Bible and turn to a certain page. At this point I had developed clairaudience, the ability to hear through my spiritual ears. Spirit voices come through clearly and audibly. I complied and came to the passage in Deuteronomy where the Hebrews were enjoined from spiritual intercourse or calling on familiar spirits. To a Jew these things are forbidden.

My sense of curiosity was aroused. I asked why I was requested to read the injunction and who my visitor was. He told me that he was a Jew and it was incumbent upon him to remind me that I was taking part in a prohibited act.

My rejoinder that the Jewish prophets and scholars had indulged in the practice was met with a silence. They were

14

prophets, I added. What stopped me from becoming a prophet? This went unanswered too, except for a repeated warning about the Biblical injunction.

During the various stages of development, a medium acquires clairvoyance and clairaudience. It was my good fortune, in addition, to learn to communicate through thought—the art referred to as mental telepathy. The occasion presented an opportunity to test this attribute and I requested that we both stop speaking for a moment, so I could read his thoughts. Surprisingly, I received the impression that his argument was based not so much on the Biblical injunction, but more on the fact that, in the seance room at the Riemvis home, there hung a very impressive portrait of Jesus, that the hymns sung were those of the Christian church, and that the lectures delivered were full of Christian context. I asked whether he or others might fear my becoming so imbued with Christian ideology that I might leave my religious belief and become a Christian. He admitted that it was so.

When I assured him that under no circumstance would I leave my temple, he wavered and gave approval to my attending seances. He identified himself as Elias, a Jew who had lived in Vienna and passed on quite young, and who had become interested in me.

We became good friends, and he has visited us many times and has been one of our protectors and prayer-bearers.

Another occasion that will stay permanently in my memory took place on a winter night early in 1931. My wife was attending a meeting, and I was left at home with my four-year-old son, who had contracted a very bad cold and was under a doctor's care.

Around 9 P.M., the child awoke with a terrible hacking cough. Each spasm seemed to wrench him from his bed. I became frightened and phoned our doctor. He was away. For the moment, I was at a loss. Then, I called for the spirit doctors and asked for help.

Near the child's bed, there stood a small night table. A moment after I called for help, I heard two raps on the table and within seconds the boy stopped coughing and fell into peaceful sleep.

With gratitude in my heart I witnessed what had transpired and my attention was drawn to a large, glass-enclosed photograph that reflected the light from a street lamp located at some distance. Clearly, the reflected light was darkened, time and again, by shadows moving about the room. Clearly, the shadows were of spirit beings.

We always pray before we fall asleep. It is natural for humans to pray most fervently when in need. As we were experiencing a bad period financially, our prayers were directed toward betterment in that direction, among other things.

A number of times we saw a bright circle of light on the ceiling of our bedroom, as if it came from a torchlight placed on the floor. Our hearts would feel uplifted, since it was evidence there were friends in spirit at our side.

I have also seen faces of the earthbound and the suffering, spooks and poltergeists, the haunting and haunted, with red eyes and mocking grimaces, which fortunately I have learned to recognize and ward off.

Once someone has begun to develop his spiritual insight, he acquires a certain light, an aura unseen by the naked eye, but prominent and easily seen by the initiated. It begins to attract the good and the not-so-good spirits, much as a light draws moths of all kinds.

One evening, I felt the "call" and acknowledged it. It was a stranger. He identified himself by name as a physician who lived in the Bronx. Several months before, he had committed suicide. I well remembered having read of the name and occasion in the newspapers. I knew how he had passed over.

He told me he was lost and in darkness. He needed help. Would I help him? I said I would.

I first asked whether he believed in God, but he answered in the negative. I gave him a lengthy lecture that resulted in his agreement to think it all over and try to believe.

He visited me several evenings later and seemed to feel as if he were on the right track. However, when I asked my spirit guides to step in and help him, I was told that, for the time being and until such time as was deemed proper, the doctor was persona non grata, and I was not to have any dealings with him. This I accepted, without knowledge as to rhyme or reason, although I believe it was because he had committed suicide.

Chapter 5

Zabdiel

DURING seances I was in the habit of asking questions of various nature, which the guiding spirits readily answered. Once or twice my questions dealt with religion or the make-up of the spiritual spheres. I was told that they were not in a position to answer, but, should we have the occasional honor of a visit from Zabdiel, they were sure he would supply the answers. I heard reference made to Zabdiel on a number of occasions and was told that he came from a very high sphere.

I avidly continued reading various books on the subject. The New York Public Library offered a great many. Among the books I chanced to pick up was a work in two volumes entitled *Beyond the Veil*, by the Reverend Owen Vale of England. He was an English minister whose wife began to work with a "planchette," the old-time version of our present-day Ouija board. Little by little, the minister found himself joining her until both of them acquired clairaudience.

Zabdiel, who had been a minister in England during his life on earth, attached himself to Reverend Vale and a friendly

18

relationship developed. The reverend tells of times he appeared in the pulpit, without a prepared sermon, only to find himself speaking fluently from a beautifully formed text that had originated with Zabdiel. A few of his congregation had even seen a benign, bearded face, above the reverend's head, during some of his sermons.

Vale's experiences appealed to me, especially because I had heard Zabdiel's name mentioned in seance. I began to wish that I would be so fortunate as to acquire a teacher-guide in Zabdiel.

It was not long thereafter, while reading at home one evening, that I received the "call." The speaker announced himself as Zabdiel and told me that he knew of my wish and would be my mentor. I was overjoyed, of course, but suspected that some misguided, earthbound spirit was playing a game with me. But at the following seance, it was confirmed to me, and both the sitters and spiritual guides felicitated me on my good fortune.

It has been many years since that time and during these years Zabdiel has been my teacher, guide, brother, and dear friend all wrapped in one. His love for my family and myself cannot be measured. No father or mother could give more, and we bless the day he entered our lives. Between Zabdiel and Rainbow, our darkest moments have been lightened and our paths become guided lanes.

In addition, we had Elias and Ahab, who shall be mentioned later, a great many relatives who have passed over, and numerous guardians and protectors. Life, for us, became a bit complex. On the one hand, we lived the life of average citizens, faced by all life's problems and ever fearful of what the future had in store. On the other hand, we gained entry into the spiritual realm, where love and life abound and where cares are shed. Here we were joined in prayer and encouraged in our prospect.

Whatever else is true, it cannot be denied that any uplift in moments of weighty darkness is worthy of thought and credence. Faith and trust come hard to the needy.

Chapter 6

A Sad
Falling Out

MY BROTHER and I continued to attend developing class at the Riemvis' home. Progress continued for all the sitters and the seances advanced to the point where partial materialization was realized. A hand would materialize out of nowhere and, controlled by one of the attendant spirits, would pat a sitter on the knee or shoulder, or shake one's hand.

It felt cool and clammy. It would demonstrate almost unbelievable physical strength by lifting a chair or a table, then suddenly vanish into thin air.

Each of the sitters was able to receive spiritual messages and to transmit them, and both Fred and Louisa Riemvis seemed to have gained a great deal of power and vision.

We have sat with numerous mediums since that time, but never have we experienced the satisfaction, the well-being, the power and strength that we felt with Fred and Louisa Riemvis.

As is natural, we invited brothers, sisters and friends to their seances and heard skeptical comments about unseen wires or strings or hands manipulating objects. To prove it otherwise, we arranged to hold a seance at my brother's house at which it would be impossible to prepare, in advance, any artificial means. We had eighteen or twenty people present.

After the usual prayer and songs, Fred Riemvis sank into trance. His vocal cords came under control of his spirit guide and several speakers delivered lectures or messages.

A trumpet with its luminous band rose, and through it a voice announced that Nungesser, formerly a pilot who was drowned in the Atlantic Ocean during an unsuccessful flight from Paris to New York, controlled it. He made it fly around the room, tapping the ceiling, which was twelve feet high, and produce the noise of an airplane motor.

Someone in the room must have snickered, because one of the guides, speaking through Fred, instructed the sitters to slowly count to ten, put the lights on, obtain some rope and tie and gag Fred securely. This was done. A long rope was used and Fred's feet lifted from the floor and tied to the chair. A gag went into his mouth almost choking him, and his hands were tied. All was done, examined and declared satisfactory. Louisa's hands were held by sitters on both sides of her. The lights were again extinguished and the trumpet resumed its feat, with even more power and noise than before.

Once again we were asked to slowly count to ten and put the lights on. When the room came to light, there sat Fred, completely at ease, without gag or rope, which lay neatly coiled at his feet. He may have been only Fred Riemvis, the printer, but he seemed like Harry Houdini.

Unfortunately, during the winter months of 1931, Louisa Riemvis declared that she intended to rent a small hall and establish a spiritualist church open to the general public. She felt that, for her ten or twelve years of study, development and private practice, she had received very little in the way of monetary return. It was time that she earned some appreciable income from her teaching.

My brother and I opposed her plan. Our contention was that spiritualism was too lofty and holy to put into a market-stall. The fact that others made money from it did not point the way for her. To commercialize it was to prostitute it, and the results might prove contrary to expectation.

But Louisa was adamant. I warned her of the danger of catering to the curious or the doubters and of incurring the displeasure of her guides, who might step aside only to be replaced by weaker or earthbound spirits. I could not prevail.

She rented a small hall and I helped with the cleaning, painting and other necessary preparation, but my heart was not in it. I felt that it was the end of the developing class and all the good progress we had made. Her stubborn refusal to listen to reason clearly pointed to a definite cleavage.

The opening of the church took place on a Sunday afternoon. Accompanied by my wife, I attended the services. After song and prayer, Louisa took the platform and gave messages to most of the people present. She was equal to the task and capable of performing it, but we felt a definite absence of the holiness and uplift that prevailed at the developing class. The entire procedure seemed cold and devoid of the particular atmosphere that should reign during spiritual communication.

I had learned, in the early stages of development, that during spiritual intercourse a communicant must feel totally at ease. Such indeed is the condition created by spirits from the spheres of light. If such condition is not present, the spiritual visitors are not from the higher spheres and the sitters are in danger.

After about half an hour, I felt thoroughly let down and uncomfortable and so did my wife. We looked at each other and, as if by prearranged signal, rose and left. I never knew just what returns were gleaned financially, nor was I interested. What I did know was that I should never see the Riemvises again in the flesh.

Shortly thereafter, Louisa gave readings to two detectives, for a fee, and was arrested for fortunetelling. Sickness followed, then loss of her sight. We corresponded on one or two occasions several years later. But her health remained poor, and she passed on around 1937. Fred followed her several years later, and I have since seen them in spirit and spoken with them.

Upon their deaths, both were ushered into the light and joined by their son, Norman, and the members of the White Circle. And yet they did not seem to radiate happiness. Feelings of disappointment or disillusionment seemed to have accompanied them across the chasm. Yes, they felt better and seemed better, but gave indication that some things had been denied them during their life on earth.

A person does not change overnight. Attitudes are carried over into the next life, often to great disadvantage. It takes years, long years, to change people even in the spirit planes. To this day, I believe, the Riemvises carry a feeling of having had to undergo self-denial and perhaps of having missed many of the good things of life.

I felt sorry then and still do. I firmly believe that sooner or later the good things would have come to them, had there been faith and perseverance. I regret that I shared only the few months with them—there was so much more I could have learned from them over a period of time—and that my financial position forbade me the privilege of bestowing upon them a few earthly blessings.

In retrospect, we feel that these two people possessed a gem, denied to most, but that they did not fully appreciate it nor properly assay its value.

Chapter 7

Automatic Writing

A NEW chapter in my spiritual development opened. It was automatic writing.

Upon receiving the "call," I would be directed to sit at my desk. A small lamp with a ten-watt bulb stood ready and a pad of paper and pencil were at hand. I would then place the pencil in my hand and put the tablet before me.

Slowly I would begin to sink into semitrance and my right arm would feel as if someone had taken possession of it. My hand would be directed toward the paper and the writing would begin. Of necessity, a prearranged signal was established so that I knew, at all times, the identity of my spiritual control. The signal came in a drawing of a Maltese cross, a triangle, or a Star of David, depending on who controlled my person and my hand. The name of the entity would be written first, then the signal would be drawn.

The writing would be very fast. I would usually complete two or three pages within a few minutes. The tenor was lofty, the messages inspiring. The trend of most of the messages was to cheer and strengthen and this gave me a tremendous uplift.

Questions have been asked as to the sensation one feels when sitting for automatic writing. In most cases one feels almost transported from his earthly tangible setting into an atmosphere vastly different and almost impossible to describe in apt language. The best way it can be described is to say that there is no tangible feeling. There is neither chair under your person nor instrument in your hand. There are no walls, floor or ceiling. One is somewhere in a vastly different realm.

During such writing I have seen, on many occasions, various flickers of light resembling those made by fireflies. These would appear in various parts of the room signifying the presence of spirits. As I have been told, these spirits are there for the purpose of protecting a medium or a sitter.

Thus I began. It was just the beginning. Subsequently as I became more proficient, I had no need of a darkened room or my usual seat at my desk. Any quiet place, indoors or out, sufficed. Writing came easily, at the times and in the places where I was "called."

It has been the good fortune of other mediums to sketch, paint, compose music, solve numerous problems, et cetera. In some cases, the old masters like Bach, Beethoven and Schubert have finished certain compositions they had begun when living or have written new ones through a living medium. A good example is Rosemary Brown, an Englishwoman, who has been the medium for the great composers. They impress her psychically to sit down at her piano and then guide her and compose through her. The compositions she has transmitted by this means have been judged authentic by musicians and professors of music in both England and America.

In a like manner, poets, artists, musicians, authors, find that words, ideas and pictures seem to pop into their minds from nowhere and bring forth material called inspired. Robert Louis Stevenson would get an idea and, as he explained it, write for hours without knowing what he had written, only to find, at the end of such time, a large number of pages filled with parts of a story that he had never plotted consciously. The automatic writer does not grasp the meaning of his writing or its significance until he has finished and read his material.

My own sittings have continued over the years. To my regret I have not transcribed all of the written messages into my journal, but I have a large number of them, most being of a personal nature involving my immediate family. Indeed, most of the messages that I quote in this book from spirits in the beyond were the result of semiautomatic writing. Only a few, such as those reported in Chapters 3 and 4, were solely the result of clairaudience or mental impression.

Chapter 8

A Ride
on a Rainbow

SHORTLY after I first began to practice automatic writing, my spiritual hearing faculties began to improve. My inner ear grasped and heard without difficulty. But I needed further practice to attain a comparable visual faculty or clairvoyance. That is, the ability clearly to see objects, faces, forms and scenes in spiritual form and to be able to describe them at the same time.

Rainbow, my Indian guide, no doubt desirous of perfecting both my clairvoyance and clairaudience, put me through a combined exercise in a message I wrote on April 12, 1931. This message and experience I repeat in greater part, as follows:

Come with me to a higher plane and I will try to show you some of the scenes. Follow me—no, accompany me on the crest of a cloud toward the beautiful light emerging from beyond. See, as we travel higher and higher, how the light becomes brighter and brighter, gathering to itself the various hues of the rainbow. We must behold it slowly, cautiously and accustom our eyes to its brilliance.

There, to the left, we see a beautiful waterfall, wide, colorful, and its waters, creeping slowly up to and over its precipice, play to us a most wonderful music, soft, serene, all-heavenly, awe-inspiring and soothing every disturbance of the soul.

Straight ahead of us rides a knight, astride his horse, clad in armor and plumed helmet, his lance bedecked with his banner. He was one of the army of Richard, Coeur de Lion, on his pilgrimage to Palestine. Now he rides forth to battle the demons of darkness, who imprison suffering souls and impose manifold tortures upon them, while keeping them below and preventing them from climbing out of their misery or even from glimpsing their land of hope.

His fast steed carries him toward his appointed task, as if on eagle's wings, and he disappears from our view, over the ridge of the clouds.

But let us look further. See those beautiful hills. Three stand out above all the others and, as the sun stays its rays over these peaks, once again we hear the murmur of soft music, melodiously, as the rays mingle with the dewy grass of these green tops.

Beside these hills we see a beautiful lake, its rippling waters shimmering with the soft breeze, and its ripples, rolling outward from under the shadow of these hills and coming into the sunlight, assume the beauty of light and color and add their own silvery soft music to that of the sun and the mountains.

Toward the right, on top of a smaller hill, stands a castle, with the towers looming in the horizon, banners afloat. The bridge before it has been drawn up. Its owner, the gallant knight-crusader, has just gone forth, as we have seen, upon his mission.

We walk up to the summit of one of the lesser hills. To one side it drops off perpendicularly. Let us look down.

Here we see a number of Indian chiefs, each upon a swift horse, their eagle-plumed headdresses flying with the breeze. They disport themselves under the glorious sun, in their long-awaited and much hoped-for hunting grounds.

There is a harbor and a schooner lazily lying at anchor, with its sails down. Shall we see it closer? Come. Here is a chariot and a good horse. For us? Of course. We shall speedily canter down to port and visit the waiting ship.

Speedily we ride downhill, the light brightens and a strong silence greets us. Something seems to denote a strong peace—a waiting. We arrive at the harbor and proceed to board the vessel.

It seems she set out, laden with cattle, pottery and farm products, to a distant port and lost her course as a fierce gale struck her. A terrific storm ensued. Darkness, thunder, lightning, heaving billows, and screeching, churning tides toyed with the ship as if it were a mere matchstick. Dipping at both ends, alternately, she took in water until, finally weighed down, she sank with all hands, who were too weary from their struggle with the elements to launch a lifeboat.

Eighteen in number, they went down with their ship, the counterpart of which we now see, waiting for the awakening of these souls, in this harbor of peace, there to take on again the full crew and sail hence into the sea of peace, where no storm prevails—only sunlight and music to soothe those wearied ones forevermore.

Having seen these few scenes, through the good graces of our spirit friends from the high planes, we

now return toward your earth as swiftly as we rose, to
land you safely at your own fireside.

I cannot say, at this point, when or where the events actually
took place. I have no doubt that they were spiritual replicas of
authentic occurrences. The main purpose of this trip was to
sharpen my visual and auditory keenness. It was an exercise
much like practicing at the piano or on a violin.

Chapter 9

A Full Page and an Empty

MY SPIRITUAL progress was steady and unimpeded. Clairvoyance and clairaudience became second nature. The fuller realization of these attributes enhanced my being, added stature to my spiritual growth, and also brought about a new humility, a feeling of being a part of a universal plan, god-like and reaching every corner of our far-flung universe.

Here I was, truly endowed with a new-found peace, surrounded by a loving host of teachers, guides and friends, all giving in love and tenderness, encouraging me and pointing to great developments.

Eager for further knowledge, I continued to read, to search. Spiritual fulfillment was on the way. But economically, I felt myself floundering and lost. In spite of the lean years following the Wall Street crash of 1929, many people managed to earn a livelihood. Why not I?

My income was spotty, the outlook bleak. I needed daily bread and all the other normal necessities of life. The question became almost obsessing. Never a saint, I lived the average life, honest and upright. My word was my bond, my promises never broken. Was it possible that I was slated to live in penury? Were it for myself, it did not matter. But there was the lovely girl I had married only six years previously and my young son. Because I could not provide for them, my love for them might have driven me to distraction. The question *why* haunted me.

One night, after I had retired and said my prayer, I began to see spirit lights. This was not new. I had seen them many times. Then out of a cloud, a form manifested itself and, while I could discern it as a male form, the face remained invisible.

The spirit did not speak. My inner ear heard no words. But a message of some type was obviously intended.

My native caution came into play. My experiences with strange spirits at times were downright frightening. I had seen the faces of the tortured and the damned and, were it not for lessons in protecting myself and fending off the unwanted and unwelcome, heaven knows what the consequence might have been.

Here I was visited by someone who did not or would not identify himself, but whose light clearly showed that he was someone of importance. His mien was somewhat aloof and very serious.

A rather large book was in his hands and he opened it, showing me two open pages. One page was fairly full with writing, the lettering not clear to me. But as I understood it, it contained the record of things or blessings received by me and charged to me. The other page contained only a line or two of writing; the rest of the page was blank. This page represented acts or good deeds credited to my account. In short, my good deeds fell far short of the mark.

This revelation gave rise to further questions. If earning a livelihood or providing security for my family depended on my good deeds, why were others—whose dealings in business or their professions bordered on the shady, whose charitable

deeds were few and far between, and whose private lives were
hardly commendable—able to prosper? Where lay the line of
demarcation? Why was I selected thus?

At my next sitting I put this question and was told. It
seemed to be my lot to be selected for a specific purpose.
Sooner or later, I would have launched my quest for knowledge of spirit and spirit lore.

For years, I had not been satisfied with the popularly known
image of God and my quest antedated my experience with
spiritualism. To learn to know God meant that His precepts
must first be observed. His ways must be known before we can
know Him.

By following His ways, we learn to "uproot a thorn and
plant a flower along the path of life." We cannot live for self
alone. Since daily requirements take most of our waking time,
we must set aside some part of our hours for those less fortunate and find moments to cheer and uplift the fallen and the
sick and to bring solace to the widow and orphan. Having
found light, we must share it.

Thus we see life in truer measure and find humility in our
hearts. We learn to walk with God and help in His work.

Upon receiving the above, I made a promise to myself. I
would abide by the lesson and admonition. Having undertaken
to carry the lamp, I had to win my way to a brighter path. I
clearly understood that the choice was mine to make and I
made it.

I prayed fervently for what seemed a long time. Then I saw
a very bright light in various colors, a signal of encouragement,
a signal of the acceptance of my prayer.

Subsequently, on April 16, 1931, I sat for writing with Zabdiel and was told of my "covenant and promise made before
God to render aid to those less fortunate."

Chapter 10

A Dream of Darkness and the Damned

THERE were numerous indications that our spirit friends were taking a real and actual interest in all members of our family. They notified me at times that my mother was seriously troubled. Her problem—like most mothers' problems —stemmed from family affairs going askew, petty quarrels and the like.

At the earliest opportunity, I would telephone her to ascertain her trouble, if any. Invariably, our friends were right. Mother was beset with little worries. Once her troubles were discussed, however, her load became lighter, her general aspect more cheerful.

At times, I was told of an impending physical condition apparent in some member of my family and advised as to proper diet, exercise or medication to arrest the condition or prevent its ill effects. My earthly doctors rendered little service in those days. Our family members did not need it. Was this due to the ministrations of our spirit doctor? We think so.

Economically, however, conditions did not improve. I found

employment only spasmodically. A little here, a little there, but insufficient to lighten the burden I carried.

Had my spiritual experience not been so brief, courage and faith might have made me stronger and steadier. But here I was, partaking in heavenly glory on the one hand and trying to meet the gaping lack of essential earthly needs on the other—a veritable paradox. The thought of abysmal failure began to take hold.

One night, as I lay in bed, my prayer finished, thoughts began to crowd each other. Faith weakened. Doubt crept in. Fear took over. I began to wonder what happens to those who, having lived with various problems and who as a result have lost their faith, die and pass beyond.

During the night, I had two dreams, one within another. I found myself walking along a street where we had formerly resided, in the Bensonhurst section of Brooklyn. Darkness surrounded me. I seemed to be searching for the house I had once lived in. Each house I tried was the wrong one. Time after time the same thing happened. At first each house seemed to be the right one, then proved to be the wrong one.

Finally, I selected one, walked up three or four steps to the porch and rang the bell. A woman came out, looked at me, turned and went back into the house. No words passed between us. But I realized I had erred. I went to the next house and a third, repeating my search and facing the same dilemma. No one knew me. I knew no one.

I returned to the street, full of fear, doubt and disappointment. I felt completely and absolutely lost—in a place very familiar to me. What was I seeking, or whom? I did not know. All I knew was that I was alone, in darkness, lost and forlorn, bewildered and confused, without help or guidance.

How long I dreamed this, I do not know. But I awoke, completely drenched and frightened, panting and crying. When I realized I had only been dreaming, I felt relieved, yet thoroughly spent and weakened.

I received no explanation of the dream from our discarnate friends. Its meaning was left for me to surmise. The only conclusion I reached was that I had been placed in an "earthbound" condition to experience the inevitable state of those souls who are relegated, for various reasons, to the earth sphere. Generally, these are souls who depart this life suddenly and violently, or who spend their lives in darkness or unbelief, then try to cling to their old way of living. Many do not realize they are dead and continue to live as they had lived.

Contrary to common belief, death does not change a person's attitude. Nor does it turn a sinner into a saint. As we live, as we think, so we continue—many times without interruption. Deeds done or undone, hurts inflicted and oft forgotten, habits acquired through a lifetime, all cling to us and clothe us until we stand forth in our own lumination as a star or as a warped relic of dismal failure. Death is but a transitory process. It is a rebirth into another sphere.

Each human is master of his destiny. Whatever predominating characteristics are developed in a lifetime are carried over into the spiritual sphere. This does not mean that a person must necessarily become a saint—as the term is commonly or historically understood—in order to avoid an earthbound condition. We are not required to deny ourselves the pleasures life affords, or the comforts we earn by the sweat of our brow. It suffices for a person to live an average natural life, provided he exhibits some virtue and is mindful of right and wrong. A life adorned by love for one's family and neighbors, a charitable aspect and bright expectation, generally suffice to admit one to the sphere of light. This is exactly what you might think it to be—a place where sunshine and beauty of surrounding scenery enhance the living spirit.

Our creative instinct produces calm and beauty on earth as well as in the hereafter. Our attitude is in large measure the control. If our lives are spent along the lines of love, of hope, of faith, if we live in oneness with the Spirit Universal, then, although we may be unaware of it, our living state becomes filled with peace and serenity. Our rebirth into spirit carries that peace with it and we enter into beatitude.

Many people live exemplary lives, yet, through erroneously understood religious teaching, persist in feeling that they are somehow guilty of committing sins or of omitting good deeds. Natural laws that evoke natural desires bring a feeling of guilt. Even thoughts that flicker through the mind, harmless in themselves but declared sinful by some tenet or other, bring a feeling of sin and remorse and drive people to seek remission from outside sources, a remission that they should find within themselves.

The Catholic church, through confession, has brought comfort to many. Psychiatrists have helped others. But what of the many who have no access to either? Then we often have a human being, good withal but with misdirected thoughts, undergoing self-flagellation, without repose or peace of mind. Such humans, upon entering the spirit sphere, carry their guilt complex and look to punishment.

Earthbound spirits continue to haunt familiar places, to seek out family members and friends, to live in the spirit world in the same fashion as when they were on earth. The duration of this condition depends on their attitude. Kindly spirits from the spheres of light patiently wait for a change of mind. Their admonition is ever, "Call and we shall answer." But the mentality or thinking power of the individual, plus his attitude, controls the situation. To those who can think clearly and assay the situation, the condition and situation become clearer sooner than to others.

Ultimately realizing that no punishment has been forthcoming, they begin to seek the light. Once they have so chosen, a spirit friend or guide will take over, prepare them and lead them into light.

There is another type of earthbound spirit, one who has led

a life on earth contrary to good example, inflicting hurts upon others, cheating, killing or doing other wrongs. These pass into spirit and haunt familiar scenes with the same attitudes and intents, living in utter darkness. This class contains the spooks and poltergeists, the damned and the doomed. What is their end?

One thing is apparent. Whatever punishment theirs is has, in large measure, been suffered in their earth life. Their lives were anything but peaceful. They were lives of hatred, not only of others but of self. Their souls became permeated with bitterness and evil. They suffered while on earth and continue to do so after death.

The sleek, smooth gangster, the heartless usurer, the unscrupulous practitioner, however elegant and easy their lives may seem outwardly, carry their private little hells within. They are forever looking over their shoulders, wary of the law, wary of retribution from human hands or from their own consciences.

Chapter 11

The Temple of Prayer

IT IS natural to wonder about matters that seem far away and remote. Our prayers, for instance, often raise the question: Whither do they go and what happens to them?

But we must first ask ourselves: What is prayer? *The American College Dictionary* offers several definitions. Among them:

1. A devout petition to or any form of spiritual communication with God or an object of worship.

2. Act, action or practice of praying to God or an object of worship.

3. A spiritual communion with God, or an object of worship, as in supplication, thanksgiving, adoration or confession.

4. A form of words used in or appointed for praying: The Lord's Prayer, etc.

Of all these, the outstanding phrase, to me, is spiritual communication or spiritual communion. We seek to contact and enter into communication with God who is Spirit, for a definite reason or purpose. We may petition for a better state of health, for increased income, for things material, or, on the other hand, we may be afflicted with grievous family problems or beset with mental or spiritual depression, from which we seek relief. Then again, being blessed with both material and spiritual benefits, we may wish to contact God and express, through love, our acknowledgment of His bounty and thank Him for it.

It has always puzzled me how God, even in His omniscience, could listen to and hear each person's prayer. I have stood, or sat, in a synagogue and prayed by reading a prepared text, as have hundreds of others around me. How did God make His selection, from among the congregation, of those upon whom He would bestow His favor? I have also observed, as no doubt many have, that at times I have prayed with much more fervor than other times, depending, I suppose, on what my needs were or how I felt.

My greatest need in the early 1930s was for subsistence, and my prayers, which began with thankful acknowledgment of my family's state of health, invariably ended with a very fervent, deeply felt supplication for "daily bread."

During one such prayer, I clairvoyantly saw myself kneeling at the bottom of a very high hill and, as my gaze was directed upward, I saw a huge building that appeared like a church or temple. It stood on the crest of the hill and shone as if enveloped in very bright light. I realized that it had something to do with prayer.

This fact was subsequently confirmed and I was told that this was the Temple of Prayer, to which all supplications are directed. The indication was that some spirit or a number of spirits received the petitions that reached the Temple, considered and weighed them, and rendered decisions that were then put into effect.

It was explained to me that not all prayers reach the Temple. Most appeals do not have the force to carry them the full distance. Where there are intercessors, however—either friends or relatives in spirit or some other interested party who is in position to render necessary aid—prayers are carried forward and upward until they reach their destination.

Thus, my vision of the destination of prayer acted as great encouragement and, as subsequently proved, helped in the realization of my petition a short time afterward.

Years later, while in a spiritual state, I was allowed to enter this Temple and to behold its beauty and magnificence. It begins with a very large door, constructed from an intricate design of material of a color between bronze and gold. The floor is of a beautiful mosaic pattern. The walls are of solid material with extremely large stained-glass windows of many hues. The light that streams through these windows adds to the magnificence and the spiritual aura. The domed ceiling seems to be constructed of a metal in bright gold and is engraved in various patterns that complement the entire structure. The atmosphere is one of peace and serenity, and it seems as if beautiful music resounds from all sides in a low tone that awes and inspires.

It may be explained here that spiritual (astral) travel is accomplished by willing one's self to be at some other place or by being transported—spiritually—by a guide or mentor.

My impression is that, if people in general would realize the full portent and efficacy of their prayers and the utmost importance of putting their heart and soul into the message they send forth, their supplication would be tendered in an entirely different key than usual.

Some people, among them rabbis, ministers and priests, attain a stage of ecstasy during prayer. They become spiritually attuned to the God-force that is ever-present among and about us. Ecstasy can only be reached when the mind is free of conscious thought, when one has become thoroughly relaxed physically and mentally, and when one is in a happy frame of mind. The Hassidic rabbis have called this approach akin to the bridegroom going forth to meet the bride.

Chapter 12

I Received This Day
My Daily Bread

IN MAY, 1931, my morale hit a new low. I tried several jobs without success. My income was next to nothing. Scepticism took hold; faith slipped. I discontinued sitting for automatic writing and shrugged off all calls from beyond. To lighten our financial burden, we rented an apartment in the Williamsburg section of Brooklyn, at less than one-half our former rent.

In pursuit of livelihood, I tried to sell a line of inexpensive dresses to retail shops. But I was looking for another position, and in the morning I used to peruse the advertisements in the columns of the *New York Times*.

One day I found one: a wholesale and chain store company that was seeking the services of an accountant to install a workable accounting system. I wrote a letter of application and received a reply. The resulting interview took me to Bridgeport, Connecticut. The job was offered to me, the stipend was satisfactory and I accepted with alacrity, although it meant living away from my family and seeing them only on weekends.

On July 19, two days before I was slated to begin, I received the following message from Zabdiel:

My son, we are so happy that we were at last enabled to bring about a connection for you, which looks so promising. That message you spoke of yesterday is exactly what we meant.

Be happy with us that God our Father has at last seen fit to bestow upon you His gift. No more burden shall ye know. He has spoken the Word and thou art redeemed therefrom

Hearken unto us—a word before parting on your journey.

Be not too hasty nor too rash in your judgments. Ease and time, reflection and consideration—these shall be your guideposts and, in following these, shall you succeed.

Let the matters that press on your mind not master your gestures. The people shall be happy to have you. Success awaits, *success* in every scope. We are definitely assured from above that your path lies bright before you. Tread it in the name of God and may future happiness—and naught but happiness—accompany you.

My task proved extremely onerous and entailed working hours beyond the usual. Planning and changes in the company's accounting system had to be done after regular hours, so as not to impede the daily office routine. A rather large office staff, with its various problems, added to the task.

Many decisions had to be made hurriedly. Multitudinous procedures required serious concentration. The impulse to rush through matters became overpowering. Our spirit friends became the "help in need." They compelled me to stop and reflect, to steer a course aimed at solving perplexing situations. Generally, they guided me in all respects.

Chapter 13

Material Plenty
in a Spiritual Desert

SINCE I HAD been born and reared in a small community, New York had never appealed to me. I felt that Bridgeport would offer an ideal combination for both living and livelihood. So I moved my family there on October 1, 1931, and life took on a brighter hue.

There was none of the hustle and bustle of a big city. Neighbor knew neighbor and stopped to exchange the time of day. Sunlight, trees, grass and fresh air abounded.

My work brought its rewards. The changes instituted in the accounting system benefited the company and brought praise from all sides.

And so, for about two years, we enjoyed a comparatively peaceful existence, with the usual small problems of the average family. We moved to a new home. Our son found many friends, attended school and grew into boyhood.

Written messages became rare. I still received guidance, through mental impression, as well as a great deal of help with any problems concerning the physical condition of our little family. Each time one of us would be confronted with illness—many times, in fact, prior to any confrontation—we would be directed to take precautionary measures, or some course of treatment, that would either obviate some ill effect or mitigate pain or suffering.

We became members of Congregation Rodeph Sholom, the Conservative branch of our religion. On occasion, I tried to discuss spiritualism with our rabbi, but to no avail. I would point out that the Old Testament offered sufficient evidence of spirit communication, beginning with Abraham and continuing through Moses, King Saul and the prophets—but I got nowhere. Our rabbi would merely smile, shrug his shoulders and close the subject.

Our search for a proficient medium, a development class or a group sitting also proved fruitless. The few mediums we contacted proved so weak and ineffective that we resolved to confine our sittings and communication to our own home and our own talents.

One may wonder why I sought another medium or a development class, since I was able to communicate through my own power. I was hard at work from early morning until late evening, which left me in mental fatigue. Even after arriving at my home, total relaxation was impossible. The wheels were still grinding. Mathematical figures and charts seemed ever-present, especially at times when perplexing problems sought solution.

At the age of thirty-two, I had not reached the plateau where one can successfully detach himself from his daily task and enter a composed state.

Thus, while the table furnished the best in viands, while the body was amply clad, while all tangible blessings abounded, the spirit hungered. I felt the lack of communication with our spirit friends and sought to fill the void by searching afield—seeking an oasis in the desert.

Chapter 14

A Birth and a Death

IN MAY, 1932, we received a message from our guides, telling us that we should give some thought to adding another child to our little family. We were told that each human being constitutes a ray in the heavenly crown. If, upon our demise, we eliminated two rays and left only one, we would be remiss in our obligation.

We had had thoughts of another baby over the years but had been stopped by our economic situation. Now, having found our niche, our big problem behind us, our faith restored and strengthened, taking note of the gentle prod, we replied "Amen."

My wife's pregnancy was easy. The expected time of arrival was early February, 1933.

Since funds were still not overly abundant, we asked my mother whether she would come to Bridgeport for a week or so to stay with my son and myself while my wife was confined to the hospital. She came for a brief visit about the middle of January.

She was then seventy years young and I say "young" ad-
visedly. She was extremely pretty, with a small fine face, hair
not yet gray and blue eyes atwinkle and full of mischief. Short
of stature and full of vivacity, she possessed a sense of humor
far above the average.

The few days she spent with us still linger in our memories.
She took full sway in the kitchen, prepared our food and
served it with great pride. After dinner, all of us attended to
the dishes. Then our evening's festivities began—usually filled
with oft-told tales of past incidents in our lives, especially those
that seemed utterly humorous. To say that we laughed would
be a gross understatement. We simply roared.

Within a few days, my mother left, full of plans to return in
early February. I did not know I would never see her again on
this earth. Yet within three weeks, I received a telephone call
from Brooklyn and was told that, while she had been eating
chicken broth, a small piece of chicken bone had stuck in her
throat, that she had tried to dislodge it with her finger and that,
for whatever reason, streptococcus had set in with accompanying fever. She had been rushed to a hospital and no visiting
was allowed.

Modern antibiotics had not been discovered and, by the
time I reached the hospital, mother had gone beyond. We had
received neither warning nor premonition. Unlike certain other
mediums, we have never been warned of the impending death
of any member of our immediate families. Why? We do not
know.

Mother's body was interred on a Friday morning. That evening, her spirit visited the entire family at the home of one of
my sisters, where we had gathered to observe the mourning
period. Through my brother Sam, she spoke with each of her
seven children, counseling each in turn. Above all, she asked us
not to mourn, since she was not dead, but very much alive and
with us.

Our mother had been an ardent believer, had sat in seances many times and, at every opportunity, had asked for "messages." She had even inquired about the spiritual spheres and about her future home. She was fully acquainted with what lay before her and prepared for the life eternal.

Thus, when her silver cord was severed, her entrance into the sphere of light was instant. She was received by her father and other relatives who had preceded her.

We arrive in the spirit plane in the same condition that we leave the earth plane. Pain goes with us to some degree, as do other physical disabilities. Upon arrival in the upper sphere, soul or spirit will either be placed in a medical center or under doctors' care, as needed, until the soul has been completely cured.

Mother received healing for two months. During this period, she visited and spoke with us quite often.

On February 14, 1933, at noontime, my wife began to feel labor pains. Later that afternoon I brought her to the hospital. When I registered her at the desk, the nurse in charge asked whether I wanted a son or daughter. I told her that it was a girl, that she would weigh almost seven pounds, enter this world around 10 P.M., and have a normal and easy birth. The baby's name was to be Pearl, the same as my mother's.

I left the hospital and instructed the nurse to call me at 10. She was certain of my being wrong on all counts and we made a wager. She lost. She called me at 10 and confirmed all I had told her.

During my wife's pregnancy, I had been shown the baby clairvoyantly and had given my wife a complete description of her. Here we had living proof of clairvoyance.

Chapter 15

Darkness
in December

MY EMPLOYER went bankrupt in December, 1933. Court-appointed receivers took over and my job was gone.

Fortunately, we had saved a little money and our problem was not immediate. The future, however, loomed dark. Our life was circumscribed, friends few, prospects nonexistent. Once again the large and looming question: What to do? To return to Brooklyn was unthinkable, yet seemed practical. Then in December and January I received two written messages. The first was:

Blessed indeed is one who seeketh and findeth, for to seek is one matter, but to be endowed with the wisdom of seeking at the right source—that is another. It is said, "Seek and thou shalt find," but there should be added a postscript. Seek at the proper source, for where there is light, there is also knowledge.

Spiritual light is as necessary for peace of the soul as

our daily bread. Without it is to wander in darkness
and to batter your head against the many obstacles that
lie in the path of all.

Seek me out, said the Lord Our God, and ye shalt
find me everywhere.

And so when ye call upon us, as your friends, to impart a thought, to counsel and guide you—ah, how can
we fail? We hasten to acknowledge our dear one's wish
and having acknowledged it we shall point the way out
of the darkness.

While it may be growing dark about us, the sun
shineth beyond the horizon. As the stars show their
gleaming orbs above your head, as clear as the skies
glimmer over the world, as definite as the periods of
day and night, so shall the sun return on the morrow to
warm and soothe and light the path for you to tread
upon.

So be it, when darkness gathers, hope wanes and the
spirit flags. Down goes our morale—and what? We
have but to lift our head, open our eyes, look upward
into the heavens and again we behold the open space
of God's clear sky, to illumine our place, while we tarry
and plan and survey our next step.

Do not plunge, my son, for a plunge in the dark may
bring unforeseen dangers. Chasms yawn and traps
abound. Stop. Look. Listen. Hear what your senses dic-
tate. Not flight, for that is foolish, having once found a
haven to rest in. To leave it of a sudden and go back—
to what? Despair? The old job hunt? A miserable hodge-
podge of uncertainty.

Stay here in Connecticut, where many happy years
await thee and thine. Thine eyes will behold the miraculous workings and plans of our Beloved Father to fos-
ter and make real a future for all of you. Here ye shalt

find the quest for future certainty, bread, butter and wine.

Carry on while the entire affair is mixed and then solved. See what happens. No danger shall come to you, none we assure you. There will be a new arrangement of affairs. Even now it is being made in spirit for the betterment of all concerned.

Zabdiel

The second message came on January 31, 1934. It read:

I come tonight, my son, to have a heart-to-heart chat with thee on thy future career and to guide your path toward thy destiny.

Already you and your sweet wife are beginning to acquire that somber look of hope afleet. Nay. It must not be. A smile, a song, a prayer, above all, a cheerful, merry disposition is what we should like to have. Witness your old affairs and see if you are not going back, seeking out old, downtrodden paths and discarding the newer and brighter ones.

We must not look back. Shut the door upon old fears and dogmas. Reach out for newer things. Might is within reach. Power is ours, if we only grasp for it. Sleep on that for a while.

Why must we repeat, pray? Shall we keep reassuring you of our promises? Let it be sufficient for us to say that it is in you to go forward and conquer. Your future endeavors will bring success in your field alone. Other ventures might bring temporary easement, but your day's stint, for long days to come, is in books. Be thou resolved to stay with it. Shoemaker, stick by your last.

I am going to impart one thought. In Connecticut, you can make for yourself a permanent dwelling—a peaceful, noiseless living and establish your family and reach your goal—a home. Here is your soil. Till it.

My dear one, it is for us to forecast a glorious future. Come with us and you shall not fail. You have served your apprenticeship quite well. An office awaits you. Wouldst see the name on the door? None other than H. L. Stern & Company.

Not as yet, but soon enough. Follow your impressions, but strive after your bread in your fashion and by the efforts which have taken you so many years to ripen into the knowledge you now command.

So onward with the quest. We are still by your side and more eager than you to see you well established.

Make for yourself a cornerstone for the little dwelling. Reach out and grasp the opportunity about to be presented to you.

Fare you well. God be with you. Head up and follow us. We guide on, now and always. All of us, Rainbow, Mother, Elias, Ahab and a host of others. God be blessed for so many well-wishers and co-workers.

God bless you and keep you.

Zabdiel

Such was the aid I received from loving friends. It was a signpost along an uncertain trail, pointing the way.

It is too bad that more people do not have the powers of extrasensory perception, because we all have spiritual guides and friends who are always ready to help and befriend us. If I have included many messages from Zabdiel of a personal nature, it is to show something of the nature of the comfort human beings can receive from their spiritual guides. If people will pray for guidance and if they will listen to the promptings they receive, they will gain some sense of the protection, guidance and comforting influences that surround them.

Chapter 16

A New Beginning

AFTER several weeks of seeking employment, I was recalled by the state-appointed receivers in bankruptcy and employed in a double capacity for several months. But during this period our spirit friends advised that I lay the groundwork for opening an office of my own.

Then, in June, 1934, I received an offer to represent a local firm that had acquired a company manufacturing electric wire in Providence, R.I. I hesitated about accepting the assignment, but was persuaded to take it on a trial basis. Here again, our spiritual friends guided me.

The experience I gained in organizing the accounting, production and financing of this enterprise proved very valuable. I held the assignment for several months and gave it up early in September, at which time I returned to Bridgeport and began planning an office in all seriousness.

Office space was located, furniture was bought, stationery and announcements were ordered.

On October 10, 1934, a series of messages was delivered

guiding each step and advising how to begin activities "on the right foot."

The following came on October 10, 1934:

Blessings upon ye, my son. I have come, as I promised, and will, without the long and usual salutation, proceed to continue where we left off.

I presume you have the idea in general. I am endeavoring to give you an outline and to have you follow it as closely as possible. That you can do it is my ultimate hope.

I know that you were wondering as to what sort of advice can be given to a businessman. But I feel that your response is one of humble appreciation and it is our most humble pleasure to give and give freely.

For tonight we will choose the word "poise." You know its meaning. It is a small word, but oh what territory it doth cover. To keep and maintain the proper poise is much alike to wearing the right clothing—and just as necessary, if not more so.

Walk with humility before thine God, but with upstanding, brave yet smiling, courage among men. Man mistakes humble mien for timidity and a spirit of utmost courage for bravado. Steer the center course. Act calmly, coolly, confidently and make them feel that you know whereof you speak.

Be brief, yet not curt. Speak up but do not shout. Stand up for yourself —yet restrain yourself lest it be mistaken for a tendency at being superior. Neither high nor low, but always in the safe lane, the middle course.

Zabdiel

Another message came five days later:

Be as punctual in conducting your own business as if you were working for the strictest employer.

Arrive at 8:30, no later. Enter the office each morning smiling and happy, as though you knew that something bright were coming your way on that very day.

Pray as you turn the key and pass your threshold.

Keep up a lively pace. Do and keep doing. Leave no stone unturned. Up and at them, and God will be at your side to lead you to victory. Steady yourself for a long pull. It won't be a question of a day or a month. It may take six months. Prepare yourself and keep the picture before you of a glorious goal—your rainbow which, God grant, may come soon in all its resplendent glory.

Banish all thoughts of fear or uncertainty. The puzzle of today will be the revelation of tomorrow. Get started and all will follow.

Count on us, call on us. We shall be ever-present and at thy beck.

Zabdiel

On October 19, the day before opening my office, I received still another message:

God be with you, my son, and keep you ever in His light.

May the morrow bring a new day to you, a new page in your life—one of success and accomplishment. May every prayer you have uttered bring further response so that your endeavor may be compensated in many ways.

We like your setup. It looks agreeable and homelike. You will find composure there and a pleasant spot for thought and meditation.

Act according to your thoughts, for they are ours as

well. Cast all shadow of doubt from thine heart. Go at
it like a brave soldier and meet your success like a humble, grateful child. Success comes to those who seek it
in the right spirit. It shall be thine.

May the Almighty crown your efforts with every fulfillment you desire.

Chapter 17

Hear, O Israel

I OBTAINED a first client, then a second. In the following nine years I steadily expanded my professional practice. Eventually our country went to war and war-born income tax laws, among other governmental requirements, required almost every businessman to avail himself of the services of a public accountant.

As a result, a number of ill-prepared accountants took advantage of the lack of restriction and began to serve the public. Their inevitable inadequacies paved the way for a fuller recognition of the Certified Public Accountant, whose abilities earned commensurate compensation. Thus, a more prosperous period was ushered in, along with its accompanying problems and responsibilities.

I rarely had time to sit for written messages and maintained contact with our spirit friends solely through seances held at our home every Friday evening. We had built this little home in 1938, adorned its exterior with flowering bushes, trees and the like and were enjoying the good things of life.

The time had arrived to begin my next spiritual step. Directed by our teachers, I sat and transcribed a number of lectures, the first being a set of twelve principles received on July 6, 1943:

Hearken then my son and learn:

1. God is one and over all.

2. He does not redeem any sect or religion but leaves redemption for all those who seek Him in truth.

3. To the Spirit Universal there is no choice of one religion over the other and all are His children.

4. To him who seeks out his Father, to him the Father responds.

5. Habit formed is trait acquired. To seek the Father in time of need and to forget Him in time of harvest is to deny Him.

6. Holy is His name, and taken in vain it becomes sullied as a flower is crushed under a clodden foot.

7. To add another religion is to add to the existing confusion.

8. Endeavor should be made to cleanse our abodes, for there lies the principle of cleanliness being next to godliness.

9. Reach out for knowledge and clear judgment—not for new untrodden roads. There is confusion abroad.

10. Hearken to your own innermost voice, forgetting outer calls.

11. Condemn not, neither judge, but tolerate if thou canst not love.

12. Last of all make peace with your own brethren, as Joseph did in Egypt; bow to no God but the one you were taught to bow to and in the same fashion.

That is advice, not a command; even the Father has despaired of His commands and only awaits the inclination of his children toward light and love. We cannot command, for ours is not the final word. We adjure and hope you will heed.

Harness the manifesting ideology and tarry whilst you learn. Ye might try the text and follow with Swedenborg. Thence to Loyola, the Talmud and Akiba—finally to Aristotle. You will find if you seek that Maimonides illuminates, John illustrates.

Whether or not you believe in the Son or His teachings, Jewish teachings should be taken into account.

Goodnight, my beloved son. God bless you and yours.

Zabdiel

Chapter 18

A Lecture on Jesus

TO ONE who does not believe in spiritual communication, it often appears that a medium delves into his subconscious and that what is supposedly a message from beyond is in reality the thoughts or ideas of the medium's own subconscious. This may be true at times, and the medium must guard against it and be certain of his source. My experience, in sitting for written messages, has been such as to eliminate this possibility. First, I found myself in semiconscious state; second, the writing was done too swiftly to emanate from conscious or subconscious state; third, I had no comprehension of the content until the sitting had ended and the written message was read and reviewed. A full page of foolscap took a minute or less to write—certainly far beyond normal writing ability.

Although I am steeped in the Jewish religion and aware that I subconsciously rebel against ideas that conflict with my beliefs, a lecture I received on July 12, 1943, clearly indicates that the thoughts and ideas expressed could not have been my own, that they were definitely those of a Christian and that they reflected his views in every way.

The message was as follows:

Zabdiel speaks, dear son, and greets you in the name of the Father and the Son. It was not I directly speaking to you at the last meeting, but I spoke through someone else.

Maimonides will come to you anon and will enter into religious discussion from the Jewish viewpoint. It is not for me to expound it. I will speak from a Christian viewpoint, for as Christ was a Jew and even today is considered as a high, very high, Jewish spirit, we who are of Christian faith have learned to look upon him as one of us.

Briefly speaking, Christ revolted against the administration of the Jewish pulpit, both in the High Temple and synagogues. He was ostracized by the rabbis and looked upon as a stranger, interloper and revolutionary. Theirs was the last word many times as to the life and death of a human, and here was one who dared oppose and criticize them. Due to his large following, they dared not commit unpopular action and so they had it done via the Roman legions. Judas was induced by members of the Sanhedrin to inform on Jesus, and the silver he received was not bargained for.

The Apostles, who were spiritual members of Christ's circle, preached and wrote his doctrine, and since we have no record but that of their words spoken and transmitted throughout the length and breadth of the civilized world, we are bound to accept them.

Hearken now to the first principles of Christ, the true spirit of democracy, laid down and propounded by him:

1. The Father is the Father of all, regardless of rank or station.

2. His temples and houses of worship must be open to all.

3. If it takes learning to acquaint one with the mysteries and so to gain proximity to the Maker, that learning must be open to all.

4. There is no divine right of lineage of high priests, but opportunity must be made available to all ranks and the selection must be from the most suitable.

Tithes were demanded, regardless of people's ability to pay, and those unable to were excluded from blessing and salvation. The poor were thus excluded from receiving the privilege. Education and learning were for the well-to-do and poverty begat poverty and ignorance, and the toiler begat a toiler—*ad infinitum.* Opportunity was not open to all.

Christ demanded free schooling, sermons understood by rich and poor, the opening of the gates of the houses of worship to the poor. Hence he became the pariah— the outcast. He not only differed in his thinking from the prevalent religious school of thought but he also defended the viewpoint of those who followed other religions by saying:

"There are many mansions in my Father's house."

Some like to think of direct discourse with God. So be it, if they have learned to dwell with Him and to keep themselves by Him. Others must have intercessors or intermediaries who carry their prayers in their behalf. We of Christian faith have learned to address the Father through Christ, His chosen son, and so we do.

Wherein is the difference? How wide is the span?

What cleavage confronts us? None that I can see. The Jew, if he be worthy of the title, has always been staunch and stalwart in his belief that the Almighty has chosen him for a special task. That can be debated, for even during the most glorious days of the Jewish people, were not other great nations in existence?

Nay, it is not so. The Jew has, from earliest times and since Mount Moriah, taken the veil unto himself and the oath of Brith and the vow to devote himself to the commands of the Almighty and to service to the Father. The Jew therefore began to benefit himself by the Divine Light.

When he forgot his vows and promises, the Jew, being in the Light, was therefore subject to greater suffering than would otherwise have come.

It is like our spirit science. Those who go without the Light may perchance trespass without quick punishment, yet those who have acquired of the science and Divine Light must live according to the rule.

Jesus, seeing his people groping in the dark, endeavored to awaken them to the truth and to guide them. Many have followed and themselves suffered for it. They organized outside the Holy Land and formed their church.

Fundamentally, there is no difference in our belief. The Jewish theory is perhaps the purest—yet too much on the stoic side. Were I a Jew, I should feel happy to follow the Prince of Peace—without the necessity of changing my house of prayer—for I should still remain a Jew.

Jewish law and lore, Jewish theology and philosophy, all were learned by Jesus, and what he brought forth and preached and fought for and died for were the principles of the Father, as handed to the Jews and as recorded and taught by the Jews.

Yes, our Christian Church is prone to forget its foun-
tainhead and its Jewish mother and Jewish disciples. It
contaminates its teaching with malice and its gospel
with hatred. It reeks of venom and stands, like the
Augean stables, ready for cleansing.

There are many in the ranks of both houses that cry
out for reform, but there are few prepared to lead.

It is our hope and aim that our newly begun task will
be propagated and spread. It is for that you are being
prepared. Let us, by the Grace of God, go on with it to
the end that Truth eternal shall prevail.

Yes, Harry, one God—one Father and all his children
—but prophets in numbers as well as teachers. With
their help we shall march ahead, smilingly meeting the
task, determined and happy. Naught but smiles must
show, for ours is a happy task: the service to our common Father. You, His son, shall glory in it.

Zabdiel

The New Testament, in some of its translations, holds the
same view regarding Judas as reported above. Years later,
when the Dead Sea Scrolls were unearthed and translated, it
was confirmed that the thirty pieces of silver were not bargained for, that the idea was injected to demonstrate the possible reason for Judas' perfidy. Neither written history nor other
authentic source seems to offer proof of such bribe. What
prompted Judas to betray Jesus is not known.

Many people now share the viewpoint of the proximity of
the Jewish and Christian religions. The cleavage of years past
now seems to be an areole. The broadminded theology and
pronouncements of Pope Paul VI have gone far to span the
breach and reconcile the different outlooks.

Chapter 19

Wally and Jack

OUR SON, Wallace, enlisted in the Air Corps and, in January, 1944, was called into service. The family's feelings upon this occasion can well be imagined. Our men were being trained and sent overseas. Airplanes and crews were flying over Europe and Japan. Casualties were enormous.

Wally was sent to Arizona for training as a radio operator on an Army bomber. The training period had lasted well over a year when his squadron was ordered to report for flight to Europe. Just at that time our armies were making their victorious inroads into Germany and victory in Europe was in sight.

Calls for bombers ceased, and Wally was reassigned to another bomber for duty over Japan. When he and his crew were about ready, Japan surrendered and the fighting came to an end.

Our concern and worry over our son would have been a very trying ordeal, were it not for the messages of strength and cheer received from beyond. We were assured of his well-being, his continued good health and the fact that he would not be sent across the ocean. The loving concern of our friends in spirit, our parents and relatives among them, stood us in good stead and maintained us. Courage and faith never failed us. At moments when worry did begin, spirit messages upheld us. We leaned on God and our friends in spirit, and received faith and help. We found a sturdy rock in turbulent waters.

Yet in February, 1945, sitting in seance, I was shown a falling plane, in which my nephew, Jack Stern, served as radio operator. Then I saw Jack with bandaged head and shoulder. I was told that he was not hurt badly, that he was a prisoner of war in Germany, and that he would return to his home and parents physically better than when he left.

We were in a dilemma. My brother Morris, Jack's father, was a naturally nervous person. We did not know whether to communicate with him or not.

Then in a week's time, Morris received a telegram announcing that his son was "missing in action." Unable to cope with shocking news by himself, he went to our sister's house and told her. She then called me on the telephone saying, "I have some very bad news. Morris is here. . . ."

I interrupted her and told her of what I had seen and heard. I then spoke with my brother who, while appreciative of my message, doubted its veracity. The next day I drove to Brooklyn and spent several hours with him, trying to bolster his courage and urging him to keep his faith in God.

Three weeks later, the Red Cross informed him that Jack was a prisoner in Germany and that he was well. Needless to say, my brother's faith was restored and, when Jack returned after the war's end, the entire situation was reviewed in awe and wonderment.

Chapter 20

The Return

IN THE years that followed, my contact with my spiritual friends became intermittent. Even during this period, on a number of occasions I sat for writing.

The messages I received consisted of personal items that helped to guide me and mine. But although I was repeatedly requested to resume both dark-room seances and sittings for written messages on a regular basis, pressure of business and the resulting mental strain kept me from doing so.

Then in the summer of 1962, we realized that we had missed the contact with our friends in spirit. So we decided to spend a week at the Lillydale Assembly, a spiritual camp located in western New York state. It was what we needed to stimulate and reawaken us.

Almost every hour of the entire day and evening was spent in seances, lectures and meetings. We were fortunate to attend a week of lectures given by Arthur Ford, one of the most famous mediums in the country, and we witnessed the performance of dozens of other mediums from the United States and Canada, who gave platform readings to audiences of several hundred people.

We witnessed the performance of a spiritual healer and spoke with a number of people who had received healing. Among them was a woman about fifty years old who had developed a breast cancer, been examined by medical men and told that, unless she submitted to surgery, her life was in imminent danger. Instead, surgery was performed by spirit doctors. The healing scar was quite evident. My wife saw it.

Another outstanding case involved a woman of forty-two, a victim of leukemia, who had been cured by spirit doctors. She later had undergone examination by medical men and been pronounced "cured," to their amazement. This lady made quite a ceremony of showing everyone a box, about a foot square in size, filled with bottles of medicine and boxes of pills, which she subsequently threw into a trash barrel.

A number of other people attested to cures they had experienced and their stories sounded almost fantastic.

My wife had been bothered by pains in her sides for quite a long period. So she made it her business to undergo daily treatment by a spiritual healer in a building called the Temple of Healing. After three or four treatments, her pain left her completely.

As a result of our week's stay, we realized more fully what we had neglected and how incomplete our lives seemed without spiritual nourishment. We decided to make a comeback and we did.

To begin with I became a member of the Spiritual Frontiers Fellowship, whose function is to spread the knowledge. This association works mostly with Protestant ministers but also includes Catholic priests, *sub rosa*, and rabbis.

These religious leaders are taught and trained to heal their congregants through prayer and the "laying on of hands." The number of these healers is growing, slowly now, but expectations are that the movement will develop.

Chapter 21

An Evaluation

MY REAWAKENING spurred me to read *Human Personality and Its Survival of Bodily Death*, two thick volumes by Frederic Myers, a psychologist and philosopher, *Phantasms of the Living*, by Edmund Gurney, various parts of the Old and New Testament, other writings on spiritualism and books by and about internationally known spiritual healers.

My eyes were reopened and my mind vividly refreshed. I subscribed to several publications, both American and British, to keep myself currently informed. I also added various books by Greek, Egyptian and Hindu authors to my library, and I reread books by the Jewish Hasidic mystics Martin Buber and Abraham Heschel. The more I read, analyzed and contemplated, the more my mind absorbed, my heart responded and my spirit soared.

In December, 1962, my wife and I attended a lecture delivered by Abraham Heschel at our synagogue. Heschel, who has since died, was then a professor at the Jewish Seminary of America and a mystic. Having read his books, I wanted to hear him. The surprise of the evening was the very large crowd that attended the lecture.

The following Sunday evening there was a general discussion of the lecture. Our rabbi had asked me to serve on the discussion panel.

I called attention to the large attendance and pointed out that there is a terrifying spiritual hunger abroad that our churches and synagogues have not sated; that in the midst of a cold war, talk of annihilation by atomic bombs, restlessness in business and the vexing problems of rearing children, people have been forced to resort to drugs, alcohol and other palliatives; that mental pressure has caused ulcers, heart trouble and many deaths at an early age; that psychiatrists' offices, hospitals and sanatoria are all overcrowded; that divorces have increased at an appalling rate; and that church attendance has sunk to its lowest ebb.

People who think about these conditions seek both reason and remedy. Although they have tried to find God in their houses of worship, they have failed. Trite and outworn sermons, covering everything from politics to book reviews, have put them to sleep. They have looked for bread and been given a stone.

And yet the Bible contains the message. Prayers hold meaning. What is needed is an interpreter, a guide, to point the way to enlightment, to a richer life, to better health, to peace of mind, to God.

Why have our ministers, priests and rabbis fallen down on the job? Do they really possess the knowledge and the ability to transmit it to others? Or like their congregations, have they made their goal material gain and publicity?

The twentieth century has brought higher education to many more people. They have learned to think and reason. As a result, the methods of religious leaders, unchanged through the centuries, are not acceptable. The old shibboleths and dogmas are a matter of the past. Our religious institutions must modernize, and the leadership and guidance must come from the ranks of spiritualists.

Religion today must step forth alongside science. Cool and rational analysis shows that there is no clash between the two. More important, age-old truths must be revealed, scientifically and intellectually, to a people ready to receive them. God's truths have stood the test of time and shine as brightly as ever.

Spiritualism teaches us the importance of worship and at-oneness, how to approach the Godhead or Spirit Universal, the way to understanding and peace, the road to good health, harmony and happiness. It shows that God's love for us must strike a response by our love for Him and all his creation.

After I had finished my observations on the lecture delivered the prior week, I awaited a reply from the rabbi or his assistant. Neither said anything. It left me wondering whether any of my remarks had struck home either in a positive or negative manner.

After the session I approached the rabbi and asked whether what I had said made any sense. He began to hem and haw and, knowing of my spiritualist beliefs, finally said: "You and your ideas. What am I going to do about it? How are we to apply this to the religious sessions, to the regular Sabbath morning or Friday night services?"

This I could not answer. But I did point out that, if he were to give thought to some of the ideas that I had propounded, he might come up with a different approach.

I mentioned my lectures, which are included in subsequent chapters, and suggested that they contained valid material for sermons that could point the way to a meaningful life and teach that death is not the end of living. I offered my time and ideas, but they were not accepted.

Chapter 22

What Happened to the Nazis' Victims?

OVER THE years we made several attempts to form home circles for the purpose of holding seances. But our attempts were frustrated. Some people failed to show up and others were tired or inattentive. The result was that these home circles were unsuccessful.

Nonetheless, my wife and I sat by ourselves from time to time. At these sessions we received communications of a personal nature from friends in the beyond. We were guided and helped with our problems in ways that saved us a good deal of grief.

One occasion stands out in my mind. Psychically, we beheld a vast number of people huddled together in darkness, looking sad and dejected. We knew that this mass of souls were those whose deaths had occurred in the ovens of Auschwitz, Bergen-Belsen, Treblinka and other German concentration camps in World War II. These souls were pitiful to behold, helpless and hopeless. We were told that, as a result of the tragic end they had met, they trusted no one, not even relatives or friends.

We asked our guides if there were a way out. They said the only help that could be rendered was special prayer. Our own prayers may have helped, because we did see some of them being led, one by one, into the light by a friend or relative. Yet the number that emerged was so small and the occasions so few that we felt something of a larger nature had to be accomplished.

So we told our rabbi of the situation, asking that, through his seminary or an association of clergymen, special prayers be given in various houses of worship to help lead these lost souls into light.

His response was negative. We could find no way to encourage those living here on earth to render spiritual help to the Nazis' victims. So we continued our own prayers and in this way were successful in helping some of our kin—cousins, uncles and aunts who were led by departed relatives into the sphere of light.

What happened to the rest we do not know. But we hope that more and more were brought into the light and helped to realize that death is not the end.

It is a sad commentary that the clergy will not accept certain truths, that they will continue in their own way to seek heaven knows what, and that they will not change unless something drastic occurs. Perhaps the day may come when they too will accept the truth, see the light and recognize that their way does not advance spiritual values or yield aid to the average human being. May God speed the day.

Chapter 23

Mediums, True and False

A RECENT article in the *National Enquirer*, a weekly newspaper, tells how the psychic Alex Tanous made a sketch of a murderer at the request of Chief Herman Boudreau of the Freeport, Maine, police department. Tanous drew the sketch before knowing who the murderer was. But as a result, the murderer was identified, apprehended and convicted.

Peter Hurkos, internationally famous medium, collaborated with the police in Denmark and helped to solve murders and other crimes. Hurkos has also been brought to the United States and has found or helped find the perpetrators of several crimes in this country.

These are examples of one kind of psychic ability. Other people are inspired to paint or to write music along the lines used by the old masters, as was noted earlier. Thus a recent issue of *Psychic News* carries an article relating how Agatha Wojciechowsky draws and paints without knowledge of doing so. Yet her art has been accepted by experts and she has had exhibitions in the Museum of Modern Art in New York, even though she never prepared or studied to be an artist.

Among the outstanding names in spiritualism are the British mediums Edward G. Fricker, Arthur Findlay, H. M. Tester and Maurice Barbanell—all well known here and abroad. We may well add the American mediums Leonard Stott and Ethel Post Parrish. And what name is more familiar than that of Jeane Dixon, so many of whose predictions have proved to be true and exact?

In addition to those named above, there are hundreds and perhaps thousands of mediums who have not achieved public fame. These people function by themselves or in a home circle or a spiritualist church and receive messages from the beyond that are meaningful to them in one way or another.

Why so many mediums? The answer must be that once a person dies, returns to the spiritual spheres and learns the truth about the everlasting life, he becomes anxious to contact a friend or relative. Thus the potential communicants are so numerous that they require a great many persons who are able to receive their messages.

So we have a number of churches, groups, mediums, and individuals who have become clairvoyant, clairaudient or both, and who transmit their messages in one way or another. Some of the mediums have become professional and work for a fee, thus earning their livelihood through spiritualism. Others operate at leisure or during periods in which they are inspired to do so. Some in the amateur ranks usually act under inspiration and, since they work without fee or recompense, are above suspicion. But among those who work full-time for a fee are many who are not above stretching the truth or adding their own ideas to what they see or hear psychically.

I know from experience that mediums cannot call on a spirit or spirit guide to come at a specific time, except in an emergency. Usually we must wait for the spirits to approach us and to signify their intention of conversing with us. Thus, when a professional medium has an appointment with a client for the purpose of giving this client a reading or message, the medium will sometimes go to some length in order to satisfy that client. I have sat for these so-called readings, and in all cases they have conveyed very little of value to me.

It is sad that the anxiety of those wishing to communicate with some departed loved one will often lead them to a medium who will make up a message or a story in order to please the customer. The worst of it is a great many people are gullible enough to accept what is not even a half truth and to find solace therein. As with all else in daily life, it is well to carry in mind the old admonition, "Let the buyer beware."

To the people who want to approach this subject with a wise caution, I urge that they read some of the many books that have been written on spiritualism. Among those that stand out is one written by a man who called himself Allan Kardec and entitled *The Spirits' Book*. Kardec was a professor of mathematics and sciences at Sorbonne University. He was also a born medium. Throughout his scholastic life he gathered material on spiritualism, and his book is a result of the many questions he asked of his spiritual guides and teachers. The lengthy book is obtainable at many libraries and book stores. This author became one of the leading spiritual lights in Brazil, and a statue was erected in his honor in the capital of his country.

I say that Allan Kardec was a natural medium. The truth is that every person is born with the ability to see and hear beyond the normal senses. But as we grow up, we become too preoccupied with the matters before us and our inborn ability is lost. But it can be regained and developed by those who have the interest.

Mediumship not only involves receiving and transmitting messages but can also include psychometry, apports, materialization and automatic writing.

Psychometry is the ability to hold an object worn by a per-

son and ascertain the person's past history, the present condi
tions surrounding him and, often, the future that awaits him.

Apports are materialized solid objects that are transported
from one place to another. They are dematerialized at the
source and materialized again when they reach their destination. If this seems hard to believe, it is well to remember that
every solid object, be it a stone, a jewel, a piece of wood or
anything else, consists of atoms and molecules that can be
disintegrated. Thus a spirit can dematerialize such an object
and pass it through solid walls, windows or other impedimenta,
then rematerialize it.

Materialization means the materialization of a spirit into a
solid body that can be felt and spoken with. Materialization
requires the presence of a medium. Regretfully mediums capable of honest materializations are few in number, and there are
charlatans who, using tricks involving quick change and darkness, pose as materialized spirits and fool the gullible.

Automatic writing is a condition in which a medium will sit
with pen or pencil in hand and a tablet before him and have
his hand controlled. Thus the writing is actually done by a
departed spirit.

My wife and I have the gift of semiautomatic writing. This
means that thoughts are transmitted to us and our hands are
guided but not totally automatically.

Yet whether the writing is automatic or semiautomatic, the
writer does not know what is being written until it is finished
and read. Furthermore, the writing comes so swiftly that a
page of foolscap paper is filled up in a minute or a minute and
one-half, much more quickly than anyone could normally
write.

Since Dr. J. B. Rhine of Duke University began his experiments in extrasensory perception some years ago, several seats
of learning (such as Bridgeport University, Columbia University, and the University of California at Los Angeles) have fol-

lowed suit and men of science and renown have not hesitated to acknowledge their interest and belief in paranormal spheres. Furthermore, articles on the subject have appeared in well-known newspapers like the *Wall Street Journal* and the *New York Times*.

Thus we are beginning to acknowledge the fact that extrasensory perception exists and our newspapers and magazines are not averse to publishing material on the subject. The most outstanding among them is *Psychic News*, which is published in England. It is a weekly newspaper that relates what is going on today in spiritual healing and other psychic areas. For one who wants to keep in touch with present-day developments, a newspaper of this type is of great help.

In addition, there are societies that can provide a great deal of up-to-date information. They include the National Federation of Spiritual Healers in England, the English Society of Spiritualism, the American Society for Psychical Research, Spiritual Frontiers Fellowship and others.

Chapter 24

Where Are We Going?

AS THE years passed, a question often arose in my mind as to where the philosophy of spiritualism was leading me. Very often my wife and I discussed the matter between ourselves.

As I used to tell her, the attainment of clairvoyance and clairaudience and acquisition of the philosophy of spiritualism, while rewarding in themselves, brought to mind Rube Goldberg's cartoons in which he would show a person going to great extremes to accomplish some athletic feat or to complete a complicated piece of machinery for no special purpose. Usually the title of the cartoon was "Now that you've got it, what are you going to do with it?" But what we had experienced at the Lillydale Assembly, especially in the Temple of Healing, finally brought to mind a proper purpose and intent that would satisfy us and greatly complement our lives. I speak of the power to heal spiritually.

To prepare myself I began to read a great deal—books by Edward G. Fricker, Arthur Findlay, H. M. Tester and others. Above all, I was fascinated by Harry Edwards' *Evidence for*

Spirit Healing, in which he cites over 10,000 illnesses, including cancer, tuberculosis, spinal diseases, disseminated sclerosis, paralysis, rheumatism and arthritis, that he partially or totally cured.

I also came across a book written about John Myers, a practicing dentist in London who devoted part of his time to spiritual healing. The book was titled *He Walks in Two Worlds;* among other things, it tells of one Laurence Parish who was almost blind and also crippled by sciatica. As a last resort, Parish went to London to see what Dr. Myers could do for him.

There, he underwent treatment for a couple of months, resulting in a complete cure. He had worn extra thick lenses, which had not aided him to any extent, and he was able to get rid of them. Indeed, his vision was fully restored. His sciatica also left him and he became a hearty, hale being who returned to the United States feeling so gratified and grateful that he brought Dr. Myers here and established him as vice-president of American Flange and Manufacturing Company, Inc., which is headquartered in New York City.

My friends in spirit also advised me to read books on psychology and physiology and recommended highly *Man the Unknown* by Dr. Alexis Carrel, which deals not only with physiology but also includes a very illuminating and instructive spiritual section. In addition, Professor Carl G. Jung provided a veritable fountain of psychological information in his various works.

I read, studied, meditated and sat for impression. I finally thought I was ready for healing. Upon inquiry I was told to "go forth and heal." So over the past twenty years I have not only healed but also begun a class to train others in spiritual healing. Indeed, I have delivered a series of lectures on the matter, which is included later in these pages. To me this has been totally engrossing and spiritually uplifting, for it seems to me that there is nothing nobler than to relieve suffering.

Chapter 25

How Spiritual Healers Work

WITH THE cooperation of my wife, who had graduated from my training course, I began to practice spiritual healing. One evening each week our home was open to any and all who were in need. Many have benefited from our ministrations.

What is spiritual healing? Who are the healers? What is a healer's function? How is spiritual healing accomplished?

The history of spiritual healing is an old one. The Huna priests in the Polynesian islands practiced this art perhaps 5,000 years ago. So did the Greek priests of ancient times in the temples of Apollo. So also did the Jewish Essenes in the time of Jesus.

Those acquainted with the New Testament know that Jesus himself cured the sick and the ailing by the "laying on of hands." The results he obtained were so marvelous that even his disciples were doubtful of their ability to emulate him. Yet he told them, "Go and do thou likewise."

Today we have spiritual healers in all corners of the world

performing this holy function. Newspapers and magazines are replete with reports of many people who have availed themselves of this means of attaining a better state of health.

We know that our bodies contain a healing intelligence enabling it to make necessary repairs or adjustments, whenever the occasion arises. Our body chemistry functions to maintain us on an even keel. If we are mindful of our needs and attend to them in proper and timely fashion, chances are that we can remain healthy.

Yet for numerous reasons, our mental or physical faculties sometimes become subject to malfunction. The flow or harmony necessary to our well-being is impeded or interrupted. Illness sets in. The ministrations of a medical doctor, surgeon, chiropractor or healer become necessary.

And I want to be very explicit in emphasizing that, when the services of a surgeon or other medical man become necessary, the sick or ailing person would be foolhardy to resort to other types of treatment. A person receiving a series of medical treatments should continue the treatments until discharged by the physician. Common sense must prevail under all circumstances.

Yet spiritual healing does exist. And we must begin our definition of it by analyzing the principle behind it. That principle is just what the term spiritual healing implies—healing of the spiritual counterpart of the body or the spirit body. This results in healing of the physical body. Thus spiritual healing encompasses an overall treatment of the several levels of human components.

We recognize the fact that there is no death. The spirit body and the consciousness live on. Once a person passes into another spiritual plane or sphere of consciousness, his character or characteristics do not change. The doctor, surgeon or psychiatrist who has passed on continues to have the urge to heal the sick and ailing. This urge brings him in contact with other physicians—generally with a group whose members want to heal the spirit. The group trains under instructors. A regimen of study and training is followed until the pupils are ready, whereupon they are regrouped and delegated to begin ministering to terrestrial patients, always under supervision.

We now turn to those who, having become initiates or adepts on the earth plane, arrive at the point where they strongly desire to help the so-called living, to relieve pain and suffering and to bring comfort and relief to the ailing. This desire becomes known to the healing groups on the spiritual plane, and the process of selection ensues. A connection is established and the healer on the earth plane receives impressions from those on the spiritual plane.

At the onset he or she is directed to a course of study, beginning with records of achievement by other healers, then step by step, to technical reading in physiology, psychology and kindred subjects. Since the healer is directed in every movement, such lengthy study is not really necessary. Yet it is very helpful to understand the human body's functions and chemistry. Even so, many have been directed to heal who are almost or even entirely illiterate. Their record has also been astonishing, again because of the effectiveness or efficacy of the spirit group.

And so, we find people from every walk of life, the rich and the poor, the educated and the ignorant, in all parts of the world, healing the sick, the lame and the halt, without recompense and merely out of a love of God and a desire to aid the afflicted. Such are the healers and such is their work, but not theirs alone, for they are but instruments or mediums working with God in a noble endeavor.

What are the functions of a spiritual healer? In the main, he is an instrument or an intermediary between the spirit healing group and the patient. He is necessary for effective results. His qualifications are: love of God, love of God's creatures, training for mediumistic achievement, a responsive nature, an innate desire to help, a sense of humility, a recognition and appreciation of his undertaking, a willingness to expend time and energy in achieving his goal, maintenance of his own good health, recognition of the source of the healing power, acknowledgment of the Ever-Presence, and abiding faith.

It follows therefore that the healer must be ready and willing, when called upon, to minister to the sick. He may be called by a sick person directly or by a third party. The patient may be human, animal or vegetable.

Healing can be accomplished indoors or out, day or night. Complete quiet is helpful, although some healers feel that music aids them and others like to use lamps with bulbs colored amber, blue or pink. In my opinion, any added features or conditions are necessary only if they help the healer.

The healer must never become emotionally involved with a patient. If he does, he becomes taut and creates a blockage. He must always remember that he is merely a conduit and his mien must be neutral, his body and mind relaxed, his inner vision directed toward a "healed" patient. He feels a current flow through him. Therefore he must maintain a harmonious, fluid condition throughout.

He functions in two ways. The first is contact healing, which involves the "laying on of hands." Generally the patient is seated on a stool affording access to the body from all directions. The healer begins by contacting the Divine Spirit with a short prayer. Then he wets his hands slightly, the moisture constituting an aid for conducting a light electric current that flows from the spirit world through him into the patient. He next places his hands lightly on the patient's shoulders, holding them there for several minutes.

The immediate effect is to relax the patient and cause him to breathe deeply. In some cases the patient falls asleep. When the healer feels his patient relaxed, he begins his real work.

Both his hands are in use. One is held on the patient's shoulder for polarity. The other or healing hand is placed on the back of the neck and held for a minute, then passed along the spine and the ribs, up and down, slowly, lightly. Rotating and alternating motions are also used.

After that the healer places his hand on the part of the back corresponding to whatever part of the body is affected or needs healing. Colds, sinus ailments, headaches, eye defects, ailments involving the region above the shoulders, call for the healing hand to be placed on the cervix, upper dorsal vertebrae or both. Ailments of the lungs, heart, stomach or intestines call for treatment along the lower dorsal region, kidneys, anus or lower stomach. Ailments of the lumbar region, hips, legs and lower regions of the body, require treatment along the pelvic region and the coccyx.

What does a healer feel when he gives his patient contact healing? When he places his hands on a patient's shoulders, he first senses rapport between himself and the patient. As evidence of rapport, the healer commonly experiences a physical sensation in the well of his being, located in the hip region of the body. Once rapport has been established, the healer begins his work and either feels heat running through his hands and into the patient's body or, in some cases, an electric vibration running through him and into the patient.

The patient in turn senses heat, cold or electric vibrations going through him or whatever part of his body needs help. In some cases, especially in the case of a sprained ankle, the patient will feel heat and cold alternately as if hot and cold compresses were being applied to the ankle. In my experiences, the result has always been positive.

How is the heat generated in view of the fact that the healer does not create it and his hands and temperature are normal? Whence does the electric current or electric vibration emanate? One must conclude that it is God's healing power that courses through the veins or body of the healer and into the patient.

When a healer works on a sickly tree or plant, he does not feel an electric current or vibration. Even so, the benefits of his healing usually become apparent almost immediately. I might add that a healer works on vegetation in much the same manner he works on a human—putting his hands on it or, occasionally, just speaking to it.

The time the healer uses on the average patient varies from one to another. I generally spend between two and ten minutes, depending on my sense of the patient's needs. In most cases both my wife and I feel the influence of those in the spirit world who are helping and we are thankful for it.

Each healer has methods peculiar to his way of operating and all methods are effective, for the healing process stems from sources other than the healer. An extremely sick, bedridden patient often cannot be touched. When such patient can be turned over on his stomach so that his back is exposed, the healer has an advantage because the back contains the heart of the nervous system. However when a patient cannot be moved, healing will still take place. Since the patient cannot be touched, the healer makes passes, with his healing hand or both hands, over the ailing areas. Such passes can be horizontal, vertical or circular.

In each case, the healer receives instructions from his spirit doctors as to places, motions and timing. He is instructed throughout the procedure.

So much for contact healing. There is another method, namely distant healing, whereby a sick or ailing person can be treated from a distance. It does not matter how far away the healer may be nor whether the request for such healing comes from the patient or a third party.

The healer reserves a time of day or night specifically for sending healing. Usually he has a list of patients before him.

Through prayer and meditation he reaches a state of relaxation. He then begins calling the name of each person and his ailment, allowing an interval of five to ten seconds before calling the name and ailment of the next patient.

When distant healing is sent at the request of a third party, the patient need not know about it. If he does know about it, faith on his part is helpful, as is a great desire to get well. But all that is really necessary is an open mind. The healer must be periodically advised, however, as to the progress of the patient. The absence of such advice generally denotes lack of interest and becomes cause for discontinuance.

God is the healer. The spirit doctors are the spiritual instruments. The earthly healer is the spiritual counterpart—all making for a team working in concert to overcome the ills that beset mankind.

Chapter 26

A Faithful Few

SEVERAL of my friends have come to me when faced with perplexing problems that disturbed them. Our conversations led to spiritual philosophy and a method of thinking that not only relaxed them but also suggested ways and means of obviating the return of periodic disturbances.

Rather than go through this course with one person at a time, I concluded that it would be more feasible to prepare a set of lectures. I convened a dozen people who had come for advice, plus several others, and began what might be called a class. Attendance began to grow and other people asked to be included. Since the audience was too large for our home, some other arrangement became advisable.

As a result, we formally organized the Psychic Universal Society of Connecticut—which was duly incorporated in the state —held election of officers and proceeded to seek a meeting place. We rented a meeting hall at the Stratfield Motor Inn in Bridgeport, announced the meeting in the papers, and had an initial attendance of about 270 people.

After our president greeted all present, he introduced me as the lecturer of the Society and I presented the aims and purpose of the organization, stressing that we were not primarily organized to hold seances or to present mediums with messages for all and sundry, but to form groups that could study with us, try for a change in their modus vivendi, and learn about spiritual healing.

The result was that we had at least twelve or thirteen applicants for membership. This, in addition to the group we already had, gave us a total of about thirty members.

We located a small meeting place at St. George's Episcopal Church in Bridgeport, and to our great surprise we were able to obtain the use of what is called the Healing Chapel. We met each Monday night and I delivered the lectures, the substance of which is presented later in these pages.

We also held healing sessions in which only two or three of us performed. In order to separate those who earnestly sought to become spiritual healers from the rest of the group, we asked for volunteers and got fifteen. We assigned them reading matter discussed in these pages.

Upon completion of each book they brought their own synopses and recited to the best of their knowledge the ideas brought forth by that book. They had also been given prescribed times for meditation, and they continued with their studies and exercises for the greater part of a year.

Toward the end of the year these people had attained the knowledge, experience, and capacity to heal and be healed—a capacity that they had achieved through example, illustration and practice. We celebrated one evening, as the pupils were tendered diplomas entitling them to go and heal.

About this time we felt that we should hold another public meeting and approached Dr. John Myers, the dentist well known both in England and the United States as an accomplished healer. The meeting was announced to the public and brought 362 people to the Stratfield Motor Inn. The evening was deemed a success, especially the demonstration of healing led by Dr. Meyers.

Our classes continued to meet at the church and we occasionally had visitors who simply dropped in on us. One of these visitors happened to be an Orthodox rabbi. He attended several meetings and during one question-and-answer period asked me whether a medium had to study and train or whether some people are born mediums and need not do so.

I answered that we are all born mediums—that up to a certain age we can see and hear clearly—but that once we attend school and more especially when we enter the business or professional world where we must compete for subsistence, these particular attributes become dormant. They generally need reawakening through study, meditation and renewed application, even though some individuals retain the attributes in full flower throughout their life on earth.

When the first year was completed, we took a summer vacation. Some of us went to Ephrata, Pennsylvania, where we witnessed performances that brought a blush of shame to our faces and chagrin to our souls. For example, I know from personal observation that some materializations were fraudulently simulated. The only meritorious part of our experience was witnessing and partaking in healing sessions that were held daily.

Upon our return, our group's secretary was instructed to send out notices of dues, a mere five dollars a person. The response was so meager that it left us a choice of either dunning our membership or discontinuing the organization.

Those of us who had been the nucleus and main support of the organization decided that it would be best to terminate it. An announcement to this effect was sent out. There was little objection.

It left nine of us who were sincerely devoted to the knowledge and principles of spiritualism and healing. We began to hold biweekly meetings at my home, to discuss current matters and developments in spiritualism, and to send healings to those who were on the several lists of the members of the group. This group, the remainder of our Society, was in reality its heart and backbone, and the sincerity and self-application of the members could never be questioned. These people were willing—nay, anxious—to do what we considered God's work and to spend anywhere from one-half hour to an hour and one-half each day or night in sending healing to the sick or ailing.

Before we commenced sending healings, each one of us gave a report on the progress of those who were on his list and were often gratified at the results and cures obtained. In a good many cases where healing was not complete, partial healing or progress was reported.

We tried to heal a number of people who were at death's door. It is not surprising that we did not succeed. Yet in a number of cases we either reduced or eliminated the pain that these people bore and brought them serenity before they passed over to the other side.

Even when a person died, we sent one or two further healings because, upon passing over, the soul still carries some trace of its ailment or disease. It is, of course, helped by heal ing spirits on the other plane.

The work goes on and will continue to go on. Even when we ourselves are occasionally in mental or physical pain or discomfort, we meditate and forget our own ills, lest we inadvertently block the inflow of Divine power. What nobler purpose is there in life than to be of help to others?

Chapter 27

God's Power at Work

THE CASES I am about to describe are but a part of our healing experience over the years. I used the plural "our" because my wife cooperated in many cases and our healing group in a number of others.

Often our ministrations supplemented those of physicians, surgeons, psychologists and psychiatrists. As I said earlier, a sincere and honest spiritual healer will advise a patient to continue the services of a physician until he has been discharged.

The question often arises as to whose ministrations succeeded in curing an ailing person. It actually makes little difference. The spiritual healer works on the premise that he heals the spiritual body while the physician heals the physical body. Thus both complement each other.

Not all people can be helped through spiritual healing. But my wife and I have achieved success in about eighty percent of the cases we have handled, and I have read that at least some other healers have achieved similar records.

Reasons for failure can be several. When a patient's condition has deteriorated to the point where he is at death's door, all the spiritual healer can accomplish is to prolong his life somewhat. Then, too, healers often face mental blocks that patients carry with them. A healer can sense this blockage and, if he is sincere, he will tell the patient that there is nothing that can be done for him and the reasons for it. Again, healers sometimes can't help patients because the latter are prone to wallow in misery and to feel a sense of martyrdom. Other patients seem to feel, either because of religious belief or some other reason, that they have committed a sin and that they must expiate it. Still others only have faith in pills, medicines and other everyday nostrums.

Needless to say, some of the results we have obtained have been called miraculous. But we do not recognize such definition, knowing that all that occurs must be within God's law. We feel very humble and thankful for our own small part as instruments in God's healing process. Now let's look in detail at some of these processes.

In 1952, long before we had begun to practice spiritual healing, my wife and I received a telephone call from friends tearfully telling us that their young son had been stricken with bulbar polio. It was a time when polio was rampant among children. Many were killed outright or crippled for life. Although this particular child had been rushed to the nearest hospital and placed in intensive care, the outlook for him was grim.

After the call, my wife and I entered our seance room, doused the lights and established connection with our guides. We prayed long and fervently for the child's health. Both of us felt lifted out of our physical bodies and transported to a higher plane of consciousness.

We prayed for quite a while and, our prayer ended, we received a message from our guides during which a beautiful, many-hued light hung suspended over us. The gist of the message was that our prayer had been relayed to the Temple and our supplication granted. We were to call the parents and the content of our message to them would be dictated during the conversation.

We called the parents and told them that the boy would be ninety percent improved by morning and completely cured within a relatively short time. I instructed them to go into silence and offer a prayer of thanksgiving.

Upon seeing the child the next morning and finding him with a normal temperature and in desire of food, the doctor proclaimed it "nothing short of a miracle." Shortly the boy was completely cured, and today he is a normal, healthy young man.

The mother of the child wrote us as follows:

Robert took ill on September 12, 1952, and was admitted to the Bridgeport Hospital that evening for observation. He kept running a temperature of about 102 degrees Saturday and Sunday and the medication didn't seem to break it. During this period they discovered that he had glandular fever.

On Monday morning he awoke with partial paralysis. A spinal test was taken and by noon they discovered he had bulbar polio. I was called and told that I could see him for a little while, because that afternoon they were going to move him to isolation. I spent the afternoon with him and the poor baby was in terrible agony. I left him to go home at 5 P.M. At 7:30 that evening the doctor called to tell us that the boy's name had been placed on the danger list and, when I asked if there was anything we could do, I was told "everything humanly possible is being done; the only thing left is prayer."

That is when I called you, Henry. The rest you know.

The cases that follow are not necessarily listed in chronological order. We recorded them at random. But they all reveal God's great healing power.

TOTAL PARALYSIS

The son of a very good friend of ours was training to be an officer in the U.S. Army and, for some unknown reason, was suddenly paralyzed in toto. The father told me of the event very tearfully.

Although an abundance of physicians, surgeons and psychiatrists did their best to locate the cause and to administer healing, they were unsuccessful. The young man continued to be totally paralyzed and unable to communicate, and he had to be fed intravenously. Thankfully his heart kept working.

We thought it best to send healing in cooperation with the parents, and we asked them to sit in a semidarkened room at 9 P.M that evening, the time we had chosen for sending healing prayer for their son. We instructed them not to pray in tears but to do their best to pray in joy and to picture their son as completely healed and cured. Afterward they told us they had done so.

Within forty-eight hours the young man was sitting up. And within another day he was running up and down the aisles of the hospital, completely cured.

We subsequently learned that, even before he had been struck down, he had had a condition preventing him from retaining his water. In fact, he was compelled to strap a plastic bag to his leg to thus eliminate any embarrassment. As he was healed of his paralysis, his water condition was also cured and today he is married, the father of a child and as normal as any other person.

CONCEPTION

The mother of a three-year-old child felt the impulse to bear another, but she could not conceive. Both parents visited several physicians and both were declared normal in all respects. The question of why they could not produce other children began to bother them to the point where it caused strife and unhappiness.

The husband told me about the situation. In order to help him make his thinking more positive, I asked him whether he would stand a dinner for four people in the event we could help his wife become pregnant. He agreed and I told him to go home and resume his normal activity.

Healings were sent by my wife and myself in absentia. Within weeks the woman conceived. The child, a healthy baby boy, was born within the prescribed time and, needless to say, the family was very happy. And we were guests for dinner.

PREGNANCY

A certain man told us that his wife had been pregnant for five or six weeks but was bleeding steadily. The doctors could not stem the bleeding and couldn't decide whether to take the fetus from her. We advised the man to wait for several days so that we could try to send healings. He agreed.

We began to send healings that evening and continued for several days. Within nine days the bleeding ceased and several days later the woman was feeling well and happy. The pregnancy was continued without ill effect and the baby was born in a normal condition, without trouble.

MENTAL TROUBLE

In early April, 1963, I was approached by a man who said that his wife had become mentally unbalanced and had had to be sent to live with his parents in order to safeguard their three children and his home itself. Group healings were sent and during May we received favorable reports. In fact, the lady returned home and reassumed her household duties.

The following December, however, the condition returned.

Absent healing was resumed. Toward the end of December some improvement was noticed, and by January a definite improvement took place.

Complete recovery occurred within a few weeks and on February 15, 1964, the lady returned to her home and today lives a normal life without disturbance.

Interestingly, she never underwent psychiatric treatment. Nor did she ever use medication except for an aspirin now and then to relieve a headache.

A husband and wife fell to quarreling, often in a very bitter, physical fashion, and were on the verge of breaking up their three-and-one-half-year-old marriage, even though they had two children. We were approached about the matter by a third party and commenced healing on November 20, 1963. Shortly thereafter, there was a complete reconciliation between the couple and a happy state was established.

Yet on January 4, 1964, we were told that quarreling had broken out again. So we again began sending healings. We continued until March 15, 1964, when a complete cessation of hostilities took place. The two were happily reconciled and today are living in peace and contentment.

A lady in her seventies had sunk to such a low mental state that she felt that there was no reason for her to go on. My wife did all she could to try to bring about some upliftment and succeeded to some extent. At least she told the lady that we would send her healing, and this seemed to satisfy her.

It took only a short time to bring about the desired result. The lady returned to her normal level of activity, made her usual rounds in a happy state, resumed playing the organ at church and continued her other interests. She still sparkles in every way and lends a cheerful aspect to all who come in contact with her.

This case demonstrates that we are all prone to depression at some time or other and that spiritual help can go far not only to ameliorate the condition but to overcome it altogether.

EPILEPSY

The mother of a young man told us her son had suffered from epilepsy for about seven years and that as time went on the attacks had become worse. Absent healing was sent, and improvement occurred almost immediately. Healings were continued for one and a half years and, as a result, the young man was completely cured. In fact, he resumed a normal life, met a young lady, fell in love and the last we heard of him he had married.

A thirteen-year-old boy had been subject to epileptic seizures for five years. His physician had administered medication without any beneficial results.

The lad was subject to the ridicule of others his age and had had to be placed in a private school. Even there he was maltreated by his classmates and had fallen into some violent quarrels. In fact, he hurt several in his class and the mother was warned that, if these attacks on other pupils persisted, she would have to take him out of school.

The mother called us and asked for healings, which we sent. For months progress was very slow and the boy's bad behavior was still in evidence. Then our group healings seemed to bring about a complete change. Although the attacks did not discontinue totally, they became less frequent and were milder in nature. The lad became more friendly toward teachers and classmates.

The case is not ended but we are looking to a complete cure within a very short time. The mother is very pleased and calls it "a change from night to day."

PLEURISY

A man developed pleurisy and suffered several years of pain

and discomfort. He happened to talk with my wife one day, and she said that she could possibly help him and explained just how it could be done. He was overjoyed and said that anything that could be done would certainly be appreciated.

We began to send healings. Yet for several months no results were obtained. Then the pain and discomfort began to ease up and within a few months the condition cleared up altogether. Today the man is living a normal life.

LUPUS

A lady was struck by lupus, a tubercular disease that affects the blood vessels and structural condition of the organs, and suffered for several years. Eventually her condition worsened to the point where she had to be sent to a hospital in New York. Since she was a good friend, I visited her and gave her contact healing on several occasions. Naturally she also continued medical treatment.

But within a month her doctor sent her home from the hospital and told her that there was nothing further that he could do for her. He said her life expectancy was very short. Nevertheless, we continued sending absent healing and the lady lived for another four years. Fortunately her last year was painless and comfortable.

A close friend had suffered from lupus for a period of years. When my wife and I heard about it, we began to send healings. Our healing group also participated in this endeavor and after fifteen months we met the man and his wife at a professional function. She told us that he was completely cured and had discontinued medical treatment and medications.

TREATMENT OF BABIES

Immediately after birth a baby developed a high temperature that could not be alleviated by drugs or other treatment.

He could take no nourishment and his condition grew worse.

We were told about the case and our group commenced sending healings. Within twenty-four hours the baby's fever came down and he began to take nourishment. After five days he was taken home in good condition. At last report he was doing well and the entire family was happy.

A newborn baby cried and took no nourishment. The doctor determined that the baby had been born without a thyroid gland.

Our group started sending healings, which continued for about two weeks. At the end of that time the baby began to show improvement and after several days was pronounced normal. The physicians could not understand what had happened, but we knew that with God's help the condition had been overcome. The thyroid gland, the seed of which might have been in the child, had come into activity and the child returned to a normal state.

AUTOMOBILE ACCIDENT CASES

While driving home late on the night of December 23, 1963, a man crashed into a cement abutment on the East River Drive in New York and was taken to Bellevue Hospital in an ambulance, suffering from a broken neck, a broken right arm and an esophagus in very bad condition. Drugs were administered and he was placed in traction, a collar affixed around his neck. Thus he lay in a low mental condition. He could get no sleep and no drug seemed to be able to induce it.

I heard about the accident on January 7, 1964, and visited him in the hospital the next day. I began giving contact healing. During this session, the physician walked in, but I waved him aside and motioned to him to come in later. Soon the patient fell asleep and I left him to sleep while I conversed with both his sister and his doctor. The doctor told us that it would

be a matter of six months to a year before the patient could be
expected to function in a natural way.

Unfortunately the patient was a chiropractor who depended
on the use of his hands to treat his own patients. In his condition, with the prospects so poor and the necessary healing time
so long, there was little for him to be joyful about.

When he awakened I told him that further healings would
be sent and that progress was expected to be more rapid. On
January 15, a marked improvement was found and on January
22, his collar was removed and he was taken out of traction.
On February 7, he was allowed to leave the hospital.

Although an operation had been scheduled by the hospital
staff, none was ever performed. The patient's neck was healed
and he had to return only for an examination of his arm.

Within a couple of months his arm became at least ninety-
five percent healed, and he was able to resume chiropractic
treatment of his own patients. Needless to say, all were happy
with the results.

On December 11, 1963, an automobile came off the Connecticut Turnpike at high speed and struck a guard rail. A young
woman passenger in the front seat went through the wind-
shield with the result that her head and face were badly cut
and her mouth cut inside and outside. She was taken to a
nearby hospital, bleeding profusely, where she was operated on
for five hours by a surgeon and a plastic surgeon. Blood trans-
fusions were given twice and drugs administered. But after the
operation she suffered severe head pains and her mental state
was at very low ebb. She was in constant worry about facial
scars—a natural fear for a young woman.

I gave her contact healing at the hospital at least twenty
times and distant healings every night for as long as she was
hospitalized. The results were astounding. Healing was so
rapid that she was sent home on December 23, twelve days

after her admittance. She stayed in bed for three days. Then her bandages were removed and she was examined. The left side of her face was completely unmarked. A long scar remained on the right side of her face, but this was healing rapidly.

Her low, depressed state was alleviated within a week. Absent healings were continued for several weeks and after January 7, the entire situation improved tremendously. Her left eye, which had been bloodshot, cleared up. And although it was necessary for the plastic surgeon to treat her on two further occasions, she continued improving and now is physically healed and mentally improved.

In March, 1965, my wife and I were at the Hollywood Beach Hotel in Hollywood, Florida, enjoying our spring vacation. One night, while seated at the dinner table, we were interrupted by a phone call from our son. He told us that a lady had been driving home from New York City to Westport at fairly high speed and had struck a cement abutment on the Connecticut Turnpike near Stamford. The car was a total wreck and the ambulance attendants needed the help of a wrecker to extricate her body and that of her grandson. She had been taken to Stamford Hospital with a broken leg, a broken arm and a head injury and was not expected to live through the night.

We left the dinner table and went to our room, where we immediately sent healing. We continued sending healing throughout our stay in Florida and until our return to Connecticut. She survived.

In fact, we visited her at the hospital almost daily for six weeks and administered contact healing. She was in a plaster cast—or rather several casts—and healing was done under these conditions.

Her neck was also swathed in bandages and tracheotomy had to be performed in order to allow her to breathe. Her head was bandaged and her eyes were badly hurt, and because of these conditions the contact healing was intensified.

She was thus treated for a period of about two months and these treatments continued after she had returned to her home. The casts were removed several months thereafter. Her arm, leg and throat were healed completely. Her eyes were sufficiently healed for most purposes, although she was warned against driving. Today she uses public conveyances. No one would even guess that this lady was almost given up for good upon her arrival at the hospital. Nor could anyone judge from her appearance just how serious her condition had been.

Her grandson was moved to a children's ward after the accident and we were not allowed to visit him. We did, however, send healings during his stay at the hospital and afterward. We are happy to say the boy recovered and is now as active as a youngster is expected to be.

LIVER TROUBLE

A gentleman was taken to a hospital in Hartford, Connecticut, and remained there for about ten days. Since he was also a Certified Public Acountant and a good friend, I made inquiry and found that he had a great deal of internal trouble and was in constant pain. Physicians could not locate the cause, however. Although X-rays pointed to a deteriorated liver condition, no definite diagnosis could be made. Nonetheless, we began sending absent healing that very night and wrote to our friend telling him about our healing and asking him to communicate with us. This is part of the letter he wrote on October 20, 1963:

I am now at home taking it easy for a couple of weeks and after that I should be going full steam ahead. There must be something in what you wrote

about in regard to spiritual healing. The M.D.s had
planned an operation on October 11, after my running
a high temperature off and on for four weeks, you
know, just to go in and look around. However, on October 9, the temperature dropped down to under 100
and the doctor told me every major organ had been X-
rayed and radiation-tested, and all showed absolutely
normal. Since the temperature was down they changed
their mind about surgery and considered me recovered.

Their best guess was that I had possibly started out
with appendicitis and that the infection shot up to my
liver and started an abscess. The antibiotics they shot
into me for thirteen days undoubtedly slowed the infection and then the old body chemistry went to work and
completed the job. This is all their surmise.

ACCIDENTAL FALL

I received a telephone call one morning from a client who
told me that he had fallen down a flight of stairs, had suffered
a shoulder injury and was in a constant pain that drugs could
not allay. He had had the attention of at least two physicians
who told him that time would take care of the situation. But he
had not slept for about two weeks and was in agony.

His wife, who had received treatment from me, suggested
that he call me. I asked him to stay at his office and went
there. I gave him contact healing and after it was finished he
said that the pain was gone completely. But he asked what the
electrical pulsation was that he had felt in his shoulder during
the healing. I explained to him that when necessary these pul-
sations will sometimes be felt by a patient.

He regained the ability to sleep and there was no further call
from him except once, when he told me that all was under control and that he was healing rapidly. A subsequent X-ray

showed that the shoulder was completely healed.

KIDNEY STONES

A young woman called to say that, because of the condition of her kidneys, she was in constant and severe pain and could neither rest nor sleep. We gave her contact healing, and during this healing she felt something slide down into the lower intestine. Subsequent X-rays revealed that a stone that blocked the passage had actually passed. After the healing the pain disappeared and she regained her comfort and ease. Further contact healing relieved the situation to the point where she resumed normal living without any recurrence of the severe pains she had experienced in the past.

MIGRAINE HEADACHE

I received a phone call from a young lady who was in bed with a migraine headache—one of a series that had bothered her over a fairly long period. Each time a headache came on, it was accompanied by nausea. But when she tried to induce vomiting, she could not succeed.

After contact healing, she fell asleep and all signs of pain vanished. The entire treatment took ten minutes and there was no trace of migraine headache for quite a while. Later on, signs of headaches reappeared, but they were minor in nature, and the lady was able to deal with them successfully by herself.

ALCOHOLISM

A man in his early thirties who otherwise seemed normal for some unknown reason became addicted to alcohol. Possibly the strain or pressure of his occupation brought the condition about. My wife had heard about it from the man's mother and sent healings for several weeks. The result was that the man stopped drinking and resumed a normal life for a number of months.

Later, however, my wife was notified that the man had resumed drinking, so she resumed sending healing. After several weeks, his drinking stopped and he began living normally again. He has never suffered another relapse.

DIVERTICULITIS

A neighbor of ours was sent to a hospital for a series of tests. This was due to a high state of nervousness, internal pains and resultant lack of sleep.

On June 2, 1965, she was hospitalized due to general breakdown and severe abdominal pains. She underwent further tests, then was sent home to rest for one week. At the end of the week her physician told her that she apparently had diverticulitis of the bowel.

On June 12, I began giving the lady contact healing and continued daily during the week when she was home. On June 19, she returned to the hospital where a new series of X-rays was taken and she was examined thoroughly. She was then sent home with the verdict that a great improvement in her condition had taken place. I continued contact healing for several days and on July 3 gave her a final healing after which she showed renewed strength and a better state of health and was able to resume the long, daily walks that she had been in the habit of taking.

ASTHMA

Several years ago my wife began sending healing to a young lady who had suffered from asthma for many years. At times the attacks had been so severe that she was hospitalized for several days running. Healings were continued over a period, and as the months passed a definite improvement was shown.

The entire matter took close to two years, but the patient was cured completely. Examination and her own feelings demonstrated this fact clearly. The young lady now enjoys a healthy, normal life and no longer suffers any discomfort or personal embarrassment.

EMPHYSEMA

A gentleman of advanced age had suffered from emphysema for a prolonged period. His physician recommended standard medication and certain precautions. But the man remained in dire discomfort, which caused his wife and the rest of the family a great deal of anxiety. My wife undertook to send healings to this gentleman and, after only a few healings, was told by his wife that he felt so much better and "is really great, and please, whatever you do, keep him on your list."

TOOTHACHE

A Saturday afternoon conference was held by the principals of two corporations that were considering either a merger or an acquisition. The conference had lasted for about thirty minutes when one of the principals suddenly began to grimace and complain of a terrible toothache.

To my complete surprise he turned to me and said, "Henry, this is where I need you." Everyone present was rather amazed. They did not know what was in store.

I turned to them and said, "Gentlemen, please excuse us for a few minutes while I take care of the toothache." We both left the room and entered another, where I gave the man contact healing. It took only two or three minutes, but the pain stopped completely. Before we left, I made him promise that he would see his dentist the first thing Monday morning.

When we returned to the conference the men in attendance wanted to know just what had happened. But he merely said,

"Gentlemen, the main thing is that my tooth does not ache and that should be enough for all."

HEART CASES

At the beginning of 1964, a gentleman came to my office to have his income tax return prepared. Suddenly he evidenced pain and put his hands across his abdomen. I asked him what had happened, and he told me that he was suffering from a bad case of ulcers and that his heart was in bad condition. I told him about healing. And although he knew nothing about it, he said he would welcome anything that could reduce his pain and help his condition.

We commenced sending him absent healing and by the end of the month he felt his ulcers greatly relieved. In fact, after examination by his physician, he was allowed to resume bowling.

This gentleman was an architectural engineer who dealt with municipalities as well as businesses. His occupation requires a great deal of concentration and tact in dealing with public officials who have preconceived notions of their own. For any sensitive person who is compelled to deal with such people, great strain ensues.

We continued absent healings and the gentleman spent another three years in a more comfortable and relaxed state than he had enjoyed in years. Although we continued intermittent treatments, we unfortunately were unable to help him maintain his relaxed state. Some of his aggravation and tension returned. Finally, in 1970, the grim reaper took his toll.

A client of mine developed heart trouble, which continued for several years. Unfortunately I did not know about his condition until I was told that he had been hospitalized in an intensive care unit and that the prognosis was not favorable.

We began to send healings and continued to for several

weeks. At this point the man was sent home and continued with medication prescribed by his physicians.

Our healings continued and subsequently the man was advised to have two pacemakers installed—one near his heart, and the other in his wrist. Today the man is well and lives a normal life. Needless to say, our healings continue.

LOW-GRADE FEVER

After returning from vacation once, I tried to phone a gentleman at his office, only to be told that he was home very ill. I phoned his home and his wife told me that he had developed a low-grade fever and that, even though his physician had given him a certain drug, his condition had worsened day by day. In fact, he was so weak he had to be helped on and off the bed.

His son was scheduled to be married the coming Saturday, only four or five days hence, and he despaired of attending the wedding. I told his wife to tell him that Uncle Henry was home and that everything was under control. Not only would his condition be better but I could almost guarantee that he would attend his son's wedding and return to business the following Monday or Tuesday. She said that was wonderful, but guardedly indicated she had her doubts.

We began sending daily healing and continued every day of the week. The result was he attended his son's wedding and returned to business two days thereafter. He telephoned a day or two later to express his appreciation of our efforts and said, "Henry, it is wonderful of you to be so helpful. You are a very good person. What can I do in return to show my appreciation?"

I told him that he was one of the few people who had ever called and acknowledged receiving spiritual healing and that the best way he could show his appreciation would be to send a check to some worthy charity. This he did.

We have not kept a record of every case that we alone or our group as a whole has handled. The reason is simple. It takes time and effort. And some evenings we are both so tired after the healing session that we need healing ourselves. So, instead of writing things down, we conclude our sessions by healing each other.

Yet even when we are tired, we do not cancel our sessions. There are too many people who need healing.

The same is true of other members of our group. Each has a long list of people who need healing, and alongside the name of each person is the malady or disease from which he or she suffers. Each of our healers spends considerable time almost every evening sending healings far and wide—certainly a worthwhile endeavor, if not a holy undertaking. We believe that, if we can reduce someone's suffering or help him or her on the road to recovery, we have done something for them and for ourselves. For as we give, we receive.

There are a great number of cases that are lodged only in our memories rather than in written records. I will always remember one case in particular.

We were holding a class in our home, and one of our regular attendants had what he termed a bad cold with alternating fever and chills. In fact, he had a high temperature, a runny nose, a chest laden with phlegm and a generally weakened body.

He had the choice of attending the session, where he might or might not be healed, or of staying home and continuing medication of some sort. He decided to attend.

When he entered our home, we were in a dilemma as to whether or not to allow him to enter the room and possibly infect the others who were expected. I stopped him from entering and took him into another room, where I gave him contact healing. Within fifteen minutes all signs of the cold were gone, and the fever and chills stopped completely. He felt renewed and rejuvenated and entered the room where the session was being held shouting, "Hallelujah, I've been cured."

This same gentleman called us one evening sometime later and told us that his young son was very sick with a high fever. He had called the doctor and while awaiting his arrival felt that he should call us and ask for healing to be sent to his son.

We sent a healing and, when the doctor appeared at the house about one-half hour later and examined the boy, he asked his parents, "Why in hell did you bother to call me when this boy is perfectly normal and without temperature?"

The man called us at once and told us the story. Needless to say, it brought us satisfaction.

To regain one's health is very much like losing something precious and finding it again. If only people would learn to guard their state of being, to watch for signs of a returning condition, and to mind habits that have been formed over a period of years, they would do much to prevent recurrence of illness and to maintain a healthy state of being. If only someone who has been ill and has recovered would keep a set of rules before him to guide him.

But to be human is to forget or to fail to remember.

Chapter 28

Spiritual Healing—
Today and Tomorrow

IF SPIRITUAL healers were few in number and considered an oddity, their accomplishments might be discounted or ignored. However, their large numbers and prevalence throughout the world have brought about different conclusions.

Men in all branches of learning are beginning to accept and investigate parapsychology. Captain Edgar Mitchell, the astronaut, engaged in a number of ESP experiments on his way to and from the moon with moderate success. These and other considerations led him to undertake a full-time program of investigation and, as a result of these investigations, which included Yoga instruction and spiritual photography, he delivered a speech on Dimensions of Healing at a symposium sponsored by the University of California at Los Angeles and the Academy of Parapsychology and Medicine in the fall of 1972. His address preceded two days of public sessions that stressed investigations of unorthodox methods of healing and borderline scientific inquiries.

Edgar D. Mitchell & Associates, a Texas corporation, was formed to bring together interested scientists from various disciplines to explore human potentials that have been largely ignored. One field they are exploring includes spiritual and psychic healing.

Captain Mitchell told his audience that he had seen instances of healing that would leave most medical men gasping with disbelief and that psychic healers can become valuable adjuncts to hospital staffs, medical clinics and general practitioners. When we learn that Captain Mitchell and other men of science have become interested in ESP and spiritual healing in particular, we cannot help but conclude that this type of healing has taken root and will grow and develop in the future.

It is worth noting that Great Britain can boast of hundreds of spiritual healers. In fact, many British hospitals now permit spiritual healers to work with patients.

Brazil has three hospitals that handle all manner of cases that are called Hospitals of Spiritual Healing. These institutions have medical men on their staffs who work with spiritual healers in all cases.

Full-time healers also work in many parts of the United States. And although they are not officially recognized by the medical profession, these men and women do help people in all walks of life.

In a June, 1973, issue of the *National Enquirer* a headline stated "Psychic Healer Helps Governor Wallace." The accompanying story told at length how a Mr. A. had treated Governor Wallace for the effects of the gunshot wounds the governor suffered in 1971. It explained Mr. A.'s method of healing and revealed that Governor Wallace has not only found surcease from stomach pains and pains in his side, but that he has also recovered some movement in his legs and feet. The governor attributes his improvement to Mr. A.'s treatment. The newspaper also revealed that other members of the governor's family and staff have benefited from Mr. A.'s ministrations.

Several Hollywood stars are also mentioned as beneficiaries of his procedure. Among them: Glenn Ford, Rosalind Russell and Don Knotts. Each willingly tells his or her story and highly praises Mr. A.'s efforts. The reason for not revealing the full name of this healer is that, if it were known, he would be overwhelmed with cases that he could not possibly include in a normal day's work.

Marcus McCausland, who is coordinator of an international study group and chairman of Help for the New Aged, a registered American charity, recently went to the Philippines where he stayed for about five weeks to study healing processes and healers.

He describes healers in the Philippines as honest and sincere people who believe their mission in life is to help others. Many of them live on the verge of penury because they accept no reward or payment for their work. The basis of their religion is the Bible and the teaching of Allan Kardec, who is also responsible for spreading spiritualism on the Latin American continent.

McCausland witnessed operations performed by spiritual healers in which no sterilization procedures were used. Yet no infection ever arose and there was no post-operative shock. The operations took only a few minutes and patients walked away from the operating table. The healers do not consider time of recovery as relevant, but they do recommend a twenty-four-hour rest.

McCausland was particularly impressed by the following: the healers' ability to open and close the body without using instruments; the accelerated healing of open wounds; the healers' ability to knit bones; almost instantaneous clotting of blood; inhibition of normal operative pain reactions; diagnoses by clairvoyance and clairaudience.

One of the healers who can accomplish these things is a

psychic surgeon named Lurival de Freitas whose record includes a great many operations and, in some cases, treatment of people with diseases and growths that have been pronounced inoperable by physicians or surgeons. His feats have been witnessed and recognized by medical experts from the United States.

In the Philippines, McCausland reports, the number of healers is growing "like mushrooms." And at any one time there may be three or four healers from other countries acting as apprentices. Hundreds of patients fly in annually from Europe, the United States and Australia to use the services of these people.

He concludes that the time is ripe for a world-wide movement to obtain recognition of what healers can achieve, so that they can be integrated into the system, not as assistants but on equal terms.

Other matters requiring study, he mentions, are the results achieved by absent healing, the spiritual awakening of those who have been healed, and the removal of obsessive entities.

In fact, spiritual healing is already under world-wide investigation. At the Esalen Institute in the United States, a group of about thirty doctors are attending a three-year course that includes spiritual development. In Italy an international conference was recently held to discuss unconventional therapies, such as spiritual healing. In Rhodesia a few years ago the World Council of Churches instigated a successful project at the Sister Buck Memorial Hospital. A traditional healer who had become a priest worked successfully with patients who could not be helped by Western medical techniques. In Nigeria, the Aladura churches use healing in their work and a Western-trained psychiatrist has twelve traditional healers on his staff. They help with psychosomatic problems because he believes psychiatric techniques taught to him in London are inadequate to deal with African minds. On an island off South

Korea, the World Council of Churches has carried out a successful project using traditional healers for the health care of 200,000 persons.

Then there is Cacilda de Paula Barbosa, who lives in Corumba, Brazil. She has gained great renown as a result of the success of her many ministrations and operations, which have been attested to by the medical profession. Dr. Romao Albaneze, also of Corumba, says: "I have seen scores of sick people visit her and leave cured. One of my patients, partly paralyzed from the waist down, was cured when he went to Cacilda. I believed he would never walk again, but he walked out after being carried in to her."

Cacilda heals about seventeen hours a day, seven days a week. One patient by the name of Joao Soares Diniz, who underwent an unsuccessful cancer operation in Sao Paulo, is now one of Cacilda's firmest believers. The patient says he was "condemned to death" before she healed him. "I came to Cacilda on a stretcher and went away on my own legs," he says.

Dr. Carlos Marigo, pathologist at the Medical School of Santa Casa de Misericordia in Sao Paulo, pays this tribute: "Her record must speak for itself. If she didn't help, they wouldn't come."

The Holy Land, where outstanding psychic phenomena demonstrated 2,000 years ago changed the world, is still in the midst of a psychic drought, relying on visiting mediums to cope with public demand. The number of healers in Israel is relatively small, but the Israel Society for Parapsychology has been formed and lectures and experiments are being conducted in Tel Aviv. Healers have come to the country in small numbers, and now healings are being performed.

Reports from Australia, New Zealand, Mexico, and other countries indicate that spiritual healing is taking place throughout the world.

Few records of achievement are greater than that made by Edgar Cayce, an American who was called the "sleeping prophet." Cayce diagnosed ailments while in trance and not only for people who were present but also for people who were at a great distance. He prescribed medication that proved proper and brought satisfactory results.

The Edgar Cayce Foundation located at Virginia Beach, Virginia, has an extensive library of many thousands of cases recording Cayce's achievements. This library is open to the public and draws many visitors.

Thus we can see that throughout recorded time spiritual healing has been practiced with benefit to many. The medicine man in Indian lore and the shaman among the so-called wild tribes of Africa have had their place among the healers and, no doubt, have been successful in healing many in their own tribes.

The fact that spiritual healing has been spreading throughout the world, the fact that it is being accepted more and more by different people, and the fact that so many healers are devoting their time and effort to it without recompense, speak impressively of this holy mission. We have no doubt that the day will come when the medical profession will recognize and cooperate with healers and bring more satisfying results to people in general.

Chapter 29

The Way
to Spiritualism

MANY books have been written by or about mediums or spiritual healers. Some outline the philosophy of spiritualism. Others tell of experiences along the spiritualist road. Some people have attended lectures on spiritualism and have sought ways and means of attaining a level of spiritual knowledge or perfecting themselves sufficiently to become mediums. Other people have held sessions with mediums—some private, some public—and have come to know the ways these mediums practice. They have received so-called readings or messages from their departed loved ones. These books, lectures, mediums together tell a story, a saga, of those who have gained fame or recognition.

There must be a purpose to everything. There must be a purpose in a story to be read, a lecture to be heard, a feat that has been accomplished or a philosophy that has been expounded. There must be a purpose to people experiencing certain happenings in their lifetime, such as dreams that have foretold the future or hunches that have guided them along some path.

There is a reason why the story of spiritualism is being told by so many and why spiritual healing is being expounded by so many healers. There is a purpose in telling the story of cures effected by spiritual healers after all medical roads have been exhausted. The purpose is to make people aware of the philosophy and the practicality of both the doctrine and the art of spiritualism.

It is important that people understand that, by living under the spiritualist doctrine, they may obtain a fuller and more serene life and a path to follow, which will illuminate their lives and increase their spiritual awareness. As we so often proclaim, the only life to live is the life of spiritualism.

For the above reasons I set out some years ago to teach people how to live under spiritual ideas. As I said earlier, I delivered a number of lectures and, under spiritual guidance, established a set of exercises that point the way and describe how to follow the spiritual road. These lectures and exercises have helped a great many.

For the benefit of sincere seekers of a better way of living and a more serene existence, I now want to turn to these lectures and bid all who read them to adhere to the admonitions presented at the beginning of each. Our ultimate aims will be to:

1. Develop our knowledge to the point where life will take on new significance.

2. Apply our minds to our bodily functions.

3. Learn the power of the spoken word.

4. Inquire into the reason for and purpose of life.

5. Search for and attain the happy life.

6. Ascertain the means of contacting God and establish such contact.

I beg each reader to live a normal life and to cease and desist from the exercises if any become bothersome. Life should be uncomplicated, and we should be allowed to live it in our own way. Anything that adds to the turmoil that already exists must be abandoned and forgotten.

I do feel, however, that what is offered in the following pages will be of great help, and I recommend that a sincere effort be made to absorb and observe all that these pages cover.

God bless you and set you on the path.

Chapter 30

Our Subconscious Minds

LET US pause for a moment and consider our daily lives. Who among us has found happiness, joy, contentment? Do we not live with compromise, accept crumbs from fate and carry a bundle of troubles and worries with us? Don't we usually accept this condition as inevitable?

Let us also ask: Is this the life we want? And what is its purpose, its reason?

Those among us who feel the need for an answer, a possible solution, begin a search, a great trek.

Yet the answer lies within ourselves.

First we must investigate the self, become acquainted with our self, know our self.

Second we must acquire knowledge of God, in relation to and in connection with the self.

Finally, we must practice and apply this knowledge to our daily life and problems.

Our search will not be easy. There is no short cut, no pill, no panacea. The quest must be comparatively slow, a step-by-step process, each step learned, practiced and absorbed. Can we do it?

Pythagoras said, "The wish to know contains not always the faculty to acquire. He who seeks to discover must first learn to imagine and to deliberate."

Thus we must bring our imagination into play. This does not mean that we must give vent to wild dreams or images, or enter into some weird method of thought-creation that may becloud reason. It simply means that, in order to grasp new concepts and ideas, we must go beyond our usual, stereotyped methods of thinking and learn to perceive new truths by mental recognition or picturization.

One factor must be remembered. *Don't rule out emotion.* You must feel.

The person you want to be is there. There are only obstacles to remove.

Bear in mind the following two principles:

1. He who gains the deepest knowledge of the true essentials of reality also acquires the deepest humility and modesty.

2. Honesty and integrity must be strictly adhered to. Consideration for others must be observed. You are not alone and you must live accordingly.

Dr. Paul Dudley White, the eminent physician who died in late 1973, tells us that man is composed of three distinct parts—body, mind and spirit. Leaving spirit to later lectures, let us discuss body and mind.

Man was created to perform physical labor. "By the sweat of his brow he obtaineth his bread."

Since the advent of civilization, the daily stint of mankind has taken diverse turns. Historically his endeavors have been either physical or mental. Yet today fewer and fewer of us are required to perform manual labor in order to satisfy our economic needs. Thus we now have an ever-increasing number of people whose livelihood depends on mental work.

With certain exceptions, the manual worker exercises his body and almost all of the essential parts thereof. His sweat glands secrete, through the pores of his skin, dead tissue and other waste material—a process necessary to the maintenance of good physical condition. He is tired at the end of a working day, and this tiredness brings on restful sleep that revitalizes him and enables him to awaken each morning, refreshed and ready for a new day.

The mental worker is denied the benefits of physical tiredness. His mind, ever active, continues to work even when the day is over. Problems that grow more complicated, as we advance scientifically, beset him, often to the point where they become his bed companions, denying him sufficient restful sleep. Competition for rank or recognition drive him beyond reasonable endeavor. Instead of being the master of his situation, he is its slave. The tail wags the dog. The result is mental tiredness, which brings on an unhealthy kind of physical fatigue and frequent violation of all rules of good health.

It is necessary to regulate our daily life so that we obey nature's laws. By breaking these laws, we invite trouble. The rules are simple and call for awareness of our needs in proportion to the amount of energy, physical or mental, we expend. Our intake of food should be properly balanced. Fresh fruits and vegetables should make up a sufficient part thereof. Liquids should be taken in liberal quantity, yet limited to healthful varieties. Proper breathing plays a most important part in our organic makeup. Periodical physical examinations by a competent physician often reveal minor bodily defects, the neglect of which may lead to greater complications.

Rest and sleep are vital. Short rest periods regularly observed several times a day are of great help in maintaining energy. They are the pause that refreshes. Sleep—the all-important function that so many cannot induce without the aid of pills—can and must be enjoyed in relaxed state. And it must be of sufficient length to allow mind and body to rebuild their vitality. Lack of sleep leads to mental and physical deterioration and usually shows up in a person's appearance as well as in inefficiency in his daily tasks.

All of us feel that we know our bodies. Yet how many of us know what keeps the body functioning properly? We may consciously try to keep fit during our waking hours. Still, how many of us give due consideration to our bodily functions during sleep? We know that our heart continues pumping blood, that our respiratory system keeps going, that our digestive system remains functioning and that our body cells die and are reborn. Yet all these physical functions remain active because of our subconscious mind.

Our mind consists of three parts or attributes: conscious, subconscious, and superconscious. Our conscious mind works while we are awake and serves all our conscious functions. It maintains our awareness. It is the pilot at the wheel, the engineer at the throttle, the farmer at the plow. It governs our seeing, hearing and working.

But even our conscious physical actions are mostly the result of experience, mental planning or memories stored away in our subconscious mind. Without memory, accomplishment is impossible. All of us do things without conscious thinking, especially minor chores that we must perform daily or several times a day.

Thus we see two facets of our subconscious mind: its roles as controller of our bodily functions and as a storehouse of things done or learned—experiences, historical facts, the past. Our memory of these things controls and guides our actions in the present. Even our planning and projection of future actions are based mostly on what we have learned in the past.

The third facet of our subconscious mind is feeling. We feel through our five senses. Whatever we feel, see, hear, taste, smell and so forth are the result of physical action communicated to our brain via the subconscious. Without this agent the brain could not operate. We would remain insensate.

The fourth attribute of our subconscious mind is emotion. Laughter, joy, sadness, tears, usually attributed to the heart, are basic emotions. We experience emotion in accordance with our capacity for it. Love, hatred, the unseen tug of our soul, all come under this attribute. Emotion overcomes us. We feel, at most times, that it is far greater than our mere selves.

The fifth facet of our subconscious is its ability to act as an intermediary or link between our conscious and superconscious, the spiritual part of ourselves, the Divine that dwells within us. Thus the subconscious enables us to look around the bend, to see the future, to receive inspiration, to communicate with those passed over or still living.

Thousands of years ago, the priests of the Polynesian islands practiced and taught that the subconscious mind is actually a separate part of our make-up that works in concert with the conscious mind. Present-day psychology confirms this. (Any split or separation is known as schizophrenia.)

The Huna priests demonstrated that the subconscious mind by itself has the thinking ability of a cat, dog or baby, but that it can be trained to cooperate with us to a fuller extent. The method used is akin to self-hypnosis. It is necessary to completely relax, then enter into conversation with the subconscious. Conversation can be held audibly or inaudibly. But the former is preferable.

Begin by telling your subconscious that you are giving him (or her) a pet name. You will feel that the name is accepted or rejected, because, fully relaxed, you will be in a position to sense the reaction. Tell him (or her) that it is your desire to communicate from time to time, that you hope you will love each other and serve each other.

Why love? Remember the Commandment: Thou shalt love thy neighbor as thyself—and remember its meaning. Your subconscious is your neighbor. Within ourselves we contain not only body and mind, but also spirit—the God-spirit. We must feed and tend this spirit morally and spiritually. It takes time and patience to attain a level of intelligent communication, but the results generally warrant the effort.

Complete relaxation is necessary. It is a state in which we establish complete balance between mind and body. We learn and experience mental control over bodily functions.

To do so, we must learn as much as possible about our subconscious, its functions and peculiar powers. We must not only acquaint ourselves with that side of our self, but also establish a close, congenial relationship with it. Having done that, we should be in a position to reach a working arrangement leading toward a general betterment of our lives. Successful attainment of this step will go far toward maintaining physical as well as mental health.

But we must also learn the hardest of all lessons, self-forgiveness. Our subconscious mind, influenced by our superconscious, becomes, through the years, a stern judge whose edicts and judgments tend to go far beyond the reasonable, sometimes to the point where our conscience persists in bothering and disturbing us at the slightest provocation.

Throughout the centuries, the idea of sin has been passed down in magnified form, so that our subconscious, in its own way, records the slightest wrong as an unpardonable sin. It is up to us to consciously convey to our subconscious the Huna definition of sin: "No hurt, no sin."

It is for us to so regulate our being and pattern of living that we neither hurt nor harm any living thing or person. If, however, we should inflict some hurt, through thoughtlessness or forgetfulness, it is up to us to make amends. Thus, we will satisfy our subconscious and rid ourselves of a burden that we might otherwise be compelled to carry.

While the conscious and subconscious parts of our mind control our physical and mental functions, the superconscious acts as the control of our spiritual being. It is the monitor over and the gateway to the Divine Spirit that dwells within us. We approach it through prayer and meditation. And when we do, we experience periods of exaltation of a magnitude beyond our comprehension or, when attentive, sense the call of the still, small voice.

No person is whole who does not unite the three parts of his mind. If we learn to pause, to become silent and relaxed, we can become attuned to the vibrations of our inner self. We can experience a new awareness and hear, see and feel beyond our physical capabilities. To this end, I hope you will try the exercises immediately following.

I have included similar sets of exercises at the end of each of the next four chapters. Each set is designed to help you grow spiritually and to increase your psychic powers.

I strongly recommend that you do each set of exercises separately. It is, of course, all right to finish reading the book. But you should absorb and thoroughly master one set of exercises before going on to the next. If you proceed too quickly before you have obtained definite evidence of progress from one set of exercises, or if you skip about from one set to another, you will retard or halt your advancement altogether.

EXERCISES

BREATHING

Place both hands across your abdomen. Breathe in and expand your stomach. Release your breath and contract the stomach. This is proper breathing, using nature's bellows—your stomach muscles. Develop the habit of always breathing in this manner. The benefits will soon become apparent.

SILENCE

Learn to sit still for five or ten minutes at a time. Try not to see, hear or think. Your feet should be in front of you, planted squarely on the floor. Your arms should be loose and your hands, free of any object, should hang loosely and separately. Breathing should be long and full.

Practice as often as possible. It is important during a working day. It makes the pause that refreshes.

IMAGINATION

1. With eyes closed, picture some pleasant scene and make the colors very vivid. See the scene well and slowly describe it to yourself in every detail. Take your time. Do not rush.

2. Think of an orchestra (or a single musical instrument) playing your favorite selection. Hear it in detail. Absorb its influence.

3. Visualize some person, even though he may be a thousand miles away. See his facial features, his clothes. Practice as often as you can.

RELAXATION

There are a number of ways to relax—that is, to reach a state of balance between the conscious and subconscious self, akin to the feeling one experiences immediately before falling asleep. Here are three methods of relaxing. I ask you to choose the one you prefer. Memorize the instructions as soon as possible. Whatever way you choose, constant practice can bring you to a level where the mere self-suggestion to relax (just the word "relax") will bring the desired result.

A comfortable chair is good for the purpose. Your feet and hands should be in the same position as for your periods of silence. Your back should be straight, but not rigid, your eyes closed.

THE CEMENT SYSTEM. *Time: 10 minutes.*

Imagine your left leg encased in solid cement. The cement is so heavy that you cannot lift the leg. Then imagine your right leg encased in the same fashion.

Imagine your left arm also encased in cement, too heavy to lift. Then your right arm. Your torso comes next, then your head and eyes. You are completely encased in cement. Your eyelids are too heavy to open.

You are relaxed.

THE SCENIC SYSTEM. *Time: 12 minutes.*

You are sitting on the shore of a lake. The water is being gently wafted by a soft breeze. Around you are beautiful flower beds, whose colors are very vivid. You smell their scent in the air.

Around the lake are mountains on which you see myriad multi-colored trees. As the gentle breeze blows, the leaves sway in harmony. The sky is blue, but here and there a soft cloud paints a pattern on it.

All about you is serene. As the sun warms you, you feel yourself completely relaxed. You are relaxed, restful and sleepy.

THE MOBILE SCENE. *Time: 10 minutes.*

You are sitting on the back platform of a moving train, watching the tracks and railroad ties slip away from you. Observe the telegraph poles flitting by, hear the clicketty-clack of the train's wheels and the faint sound of its whistle. Picture the scenery as you travel. A river with a bridge crossing it, a tunnel, fields of ripe grain, green meadows, pastureland with cattle grazing. On and on and on, until your head begins to nod.

All these methods, tried and practiced, will produce results. Patience and perseverance may be called for in certain cases. But the art of relaxation must be learned. Unless you have learned it and perfected yourself to the point where you can relax at will, no further progress is possible.

Some people prefer to lie prone when trying to relax. We do not oppose this way. However, as you continue reading this book, you will find it best to relax in a sitting position so that you may read and then take the next step and the next, learning to climb the ladder rung by rung.

Reading is a must. I have suggested certain books, but you should not be confined to these alone. Where time and circumstance allow, additional reading will be helpful.

I suggest the following books in connection with this lesson:

The Reach of the Mind, J. B. Rhine, revised edition, 1961, $4, Peter Smith; also in paperback, $1.95, Morrow.

Man the Unknown, Alexis Carrel, revised edition, 1939, $5.50, Harper and Row.

Chapter 31

The Realm
of the Ineffable

MEN'S perceptions differ, depending greatly on their attitudes, training, experience and sensitivity. Generally, our daily lives are filled with common tasks and our minds and thinking are directed accordingly. We have a job before us, a place to reach. It is uppermost in our thought. Should anything out of the ordinary occur, we let it go by unnoticed or reject it as an annoyance.

A case in point: Two men stand on a London street, listening to the bells chime at Westminister Abbey. One says, "Aren't these chimes beautiful?" The other replies, "I can't hear you. Those damned bells are making so much noise!" One is attuned to the din and noise. The other experiences pleasure or amazement.

But what is real amazement? How does it come to us? How does it affect us?

Real amazement occurs when we see or sense something that cannot be put into words. A sunrise, a sunset, star-studded skies, a beautiful symphony, a work of art leave us speechless.

How do we describe our feeling? We cannot, for most of our attempts result in mere cliches. We have entered into the realm of the ineffable.

We must see the world without preconceived notions, with eyes undimmed by memory or volition. Yet we rarely discover. We remember before we think. We see the present in the light of the past. We constantly compare instead of penetrating, and even when we penetrate it is never without some prejudice.

Memory is often a hindrance to creative experience. Our beliefs, based on memory of early teaching, impel us to try to fit all new ideas and experiences into a ready-made niche or pigeonhole. Failing to do so, we promptly reject them.

Still, some of our reaching toward the ineffable stays, persists, troubles us. Eventually it causes dissatisfaction or unhappiness. Thus we enter into a struggle within ourselves. Yet we can satisfy our pangs by acknowledging God—and then by learning to reach and understand Him.

The body is not ours to have and to hold or to own. The mind, conscience, and spirit are not our own. We merely hold them in trust. We are but an infinitesimal part of the whole. No man is an island unto himself, but part of an overall plan.

I do not own the "I," the self. I do not control the coming in and the going out. There are forces outside myself that influence my being and help control my destiny.

Who or what? Here again we reach into the ineffable, the mystery.

Why is it necessary or even advisable for us to delve into the mystery? Can we not live our usual way, without pondering over the mysterious? Why look for a headache? Aren't our daily lives enough without more perplexities?

If our lives are complete, if we are healthy physically and mentally, if our souls have found peace and contentment, we need look no further.

But perhaps we are confronted with problems of bodily

health, economic insufficiency, or absence of peace of mind. Or perhaps the small voice within us, the whispering of our soul, bothers and disturbs us. Or perhaps we do not readily accept everything that happens to us as our fate, as God's will. If this is the case, we stand forth to challenge and question. And the challenge and the question become the beginning of knowledge. We inquire, seek and read.

What have our sages said? Our forebears? What gave so much meaning to the Bible, the Talmud, the great philosophers? What has perpetuated these written records down through the ages and made them sources of deep knowledge?

All such sources point in one direction—to a universal wisdom, an all-embracing power, to our God, author and creator, the real and actual owner of the "I," in whom we live and who lives in us.

Reject that if you choose. You are free to do so. No punishment will be meted out to you. No lightning will strike you down. Yet real freedom can come only from listening to the small, still voice, from recognizing the true meaning of one's self and its relationship to the overall plan, from acknowledging the existence of the Spirit Universal, all-embracing in love.

Every person of a sensitive nature must have a set of values to live by. Among such values must be honesty, integrity, love, appreciation of music and art, religious belief, family feeling and pity. Do we acquire such values consciously or unconsciously, voluntarily or forcibly?

If you have ever watched a baby who has learned to walk respond to music by dancing, or if you have ever reacted to music or to a beautiful painting or sculpture, you must have concluded that the reaction is involuntary—i.e., it emanates from the subconscious. It is true that a number of attributes and traits are a result of early training and examples learned at home and in school, but even then the process of acquiring these traits results from subconscious acceptance of them. Once accepted, they become a pattern or modus vivendi that stays with us throughout life.

These values, attributes, traits, or patterns are therefore absorbed into our inner selves and are deeply imbedded, although often neglected. Yet they may be vividly brought to the surface from time to time to inspire, guide, elevate or point a finger at us. Have we, absorbed in some thought or problem, passed a blind beggar in the street without giving him a coin, then felt impelled to turn back or, having failed to do so, experienced an inner stab? Have we, in a moment of thoughtless anger, spoken harshly to a loved one or an employee, only to be assailed, moments later, by utter regret?

Most of us are endowed by our Creator with deep sensitivity. We feel deeply and sincerely. The way we treat ourselves and others depends chiefly on our being able to stop, if but for a second, and bring forth from our depths the Divine spark that will point us to the right path. Following the path will result in gratification and add to our happiness and well-being. Contrary action will result in misery, an empty feeling of unfulfillment, a void that can only accumulate another scar.

If we acknowledge the existence of God, we must also acknowledge that all we are, all we ever strive for or hope to be, is encompassed by His law. Endowed as he is with free will, man always has choice, and on that choice depends the results he obtains. What then is the law? What particular path must we follow to live within it?

The most important phase of the law is love. Every religion teaches us that God is love, that God loves His creation, that we, His children, are His beloved. Many will point to themselves or others who have suffered trials or disasters and ask: How can God do this to me (or to others) if He loves us?

There are many possible answers. One is that, although our Father sheds His love on us, it is mostly a one-sided affair. We seldom respond. Unlike a human who—failing to receive the proper response from one he loves—ultimately cools in his ardor and ceases loving, God's love ever abounds.

Indeed, a proper conception of Him proves that He is not a God of wrath. Look about you. Think it over carefully. Man brings misery, trials and disasters upon himself. The law of karma, cause and effect, bears inevitable results. In most cases, as we sow, we reap.

How can we respond to God's love? We can respond by meditating and pouring our love upon God, who lives in us and in whom we live, much like a lover, declaring our deep feeling in full-hearted joy. We can also respond by emulating God. Because God's love is universal, our love must be so. Like God, we must measure our lives and treat His creatures with due love, doing unto others as we would have them do unto us.

We must, like God, be patient with the ineptitudes of our fellow man. If we cannot love our fellow man, finding him lacking the qualities that appeal to us, we must tolerate and pity him for his blindness and ignorance. Thus we should not be provoked or provoking. We must forgive as we would be forgiven.

Life, being sacred, must be preserved. The hand should be lifted to help, not to hurt. Vengeance for wrongdoings, real or imaginary, is not ours to take. In wreaking vengeance, we mostly harm ourselves.

This does not mean that man should not protect himself or his property when threatened and in danger. Yet even then, malice has no place.

We should always be aware of the presence in us and about us and, being aware, guide our actions accordingly. Stop for a moment, think and feel. The ancient truth, "Be still and know that I am God," will become your watchword and bless your days.

As we create for good, as we lift a hand in help, as we console in time of sadness, as we cheer in time of sickness, we bless and are blessed in turn. We dispense His love. Our heart responds and we feel whole. We are His children. As we forgive, we dispense His mercy. Knowing this and keeping this knowledge before us, we walk in light and joy.

So then, if we stop and contemplate, we must conclude that we might as well pick up our little instrument, join the orchestra, and play the tunes God has prescribed. How? We must speak to the conductor. But we, ordinary, prosaic mortals, cannot see the conductor or hear him, can we?

Yet we must learn how to see and to hear Him, to sense Him. Spurred by our desire to converse, we have one definite method: prayer or communion.

What is prayer? It is communication.

What are the conditions necessary for effective prayer? Relaxation.

And how can we pray? Either orally or silently.

In praying we must not concentrate on our needs or our complaints. Since we are dealing with a loving Father, we must express our faith and, in joy, picture the condition, the event, that we want to bring into being. Our sincere belief that He can and will grant us our wish will bring deliverance near to us. We must bear this deliverance in mind, believe that it will happen, and thank our loving Father for it.

Do we have to pray? Doesn't an all-knowing God realize what we need? God likes to be called on and reminded that we care. God also demands that we function within natural laws and His laws.

Disregard of either inevitably brings sorrowful results, sooner or later. The animal, or imperceptive man, disregards these laws and suffers punishment, both now and hereafter. The wise man observes them and benefits.

So prayer or supplication must work within natural laws and God's laws. The Almighty Spirit will not work outside these laws. Miracles do not occur. Each happening, each event, results from the functioning of these laws.

Again: What is prayer? It is communion or communication. It is an attempt to reach the ineffable.

How do we pray? Silently or in spoken words.

Do we use our own words, or do we follow a prescribed regimen?

Either way will do. But reading a prescribed text diminishes our ability to transmit our own real feelings.

Do we have to attend church to pray effectively? Not necessarily, but church or group services generally serve to help community endeavors. By attending such services we act as part of a community and join in its common aims, obeying the edict, "Do not segregate thyself from thy congregation." Praying for personal purposes can be done in your home, indoors, outdoors, anywhere, at any time.

Let us remember that, as we pray for something to occur, we should utter prayers of thanksgiving in acknowledgment of the gift of life, our ability to maintain a fair state of health, to obtain sustenance and, above all, to love and receive the love of our near and dear ones. Each time we feel the urge to gripe, let us take inventory and be thankful that our blessings far outnumber our real or imaginary complaints. Then, to satisfy our inner self, let us make a gift to charity.

How do we receive answers to our prayers? Through healing of the body, peace of mind, abundance.

Rabbis say that we must let God judge what is best for us, because we do not perceive the ultimate good. No doubt it is often so. But let us not hesitate to tell Him what we consider to be important to us. When He answers, we will know that we have made contact with the ineffable.

EXERCISES

CONCENTRATION

Take a pencil, pen or other small object you usually carry or wear. Look at it for a full minute or even longer. Describe it to yourself, slowly, in every detail, considering its origin, material contents and function. Then try to analyze any spiritual function it may have.

Make notes if you consider it helpful. Retain such notes.

RELAXATION

Using one of the methods described in the previous exercises, relax. Converse with your subconscious.

PSYCHO-KINESIS

This is a demonstration of the ability of your subconscious to perform physically.

Take a string about ten inches long. Attach a large button, nail or other light object to one end, and tie the other end to a table corner, a lamp or other object in such a way as to allow the pendulum to swing freely. Make certain that it is not in motion.

Speak to your subconscious and ask it to swing the pendulum in an indicated direction. Then reverse direction. If no result ensues, repeat your request.

In the event your subconscious fails to cooperate, a true relationship with it has not yet been established. You must spend more time, patience and effort to bring about a better relationship. Converse with your subconscious and ask for its cooperation. Reward it as you would a child by eating or drinking something very agreeable, playing your favorite record, or engaging in your favorite sport.

THE RAIN PRAYER

If you feel tired, physically or mentally, if you are depressed or beset by a troublesome problem, this type of prayer can go far to ameliorate the existing condition or even eliminate it.

Stand erect but not rigid with your feet about ten inches apart. Stand with a wall at your back, about six inches away, because you will find yourself swaying after a minute or so and will need the wall to keep from falling.

Extend both arms sideways, keeping them at shoulder height, palms upward, fingers close—but not tightly—together. Close your eyes.

Address yourself to God and ask for the healing rain. You will feel an electric current seeping into your hands and your entire body. You will become re-energized, revitalized. Continue the stance for as long as you are comfortable, but three to five minutes should suffice.

Do this as often as you wish. It is far better than a coffee break. For the air about us is charged with electricity. The current is never shut off. It carries energy and vitality that our body and mind can use, provided we pause to receive it consciously and reverently.

PRAYER

Since the Divine Spirit abides within us, we need not seek God elsewhere. How do we approach Him?

If you read this chapter, you learned that prayer is communion or conversation. We converse with our loving Father and we must do so in a relaxed, happy state. To do otherwise is to create a block. We speak to Him in sincerity and in full expectation of receiving. No rite or ritual is necessary. A simple, relaxed approach is best.

In time of stress or grief, compose yourself as much as possible and speak from the strength that will come to you at the moment. There is no need to prostrate yourself, either physically or spiritually. Be humble, yet strong, with a strength that emanates from Him. Approach Him in love and receive of His love in return.

PSALM 23

Memorize this beautiful psalm, which is an affirmation of faith. Recite it to yourself when troubled or unable to fall asleep. Repeat it again and again until you are relieved or until sleep overcomes you. You will find it invaluable. In case you can't remember it in full, here it is (from the King James Version of the Bible):

The Lord is my shepherd; I shall not want.

He maketh me to lie down in green pastures: he leadeth me beside the still waters.

He restoreth my soul: he leadeth me in the paths of righteousness for his name's sake.

Yea, though I walk through the valley of the shadow of death,

I will fear no evil: for thou art with me; thy rod and thy staff comfort me.

Thou preparest a table before me in the presence of mine enemies: thou anointest my head with oil; my cup runneth over.

Surely goodness and mercy shall follow me all the days of my life: and I will dwell in the house of the Lord for ever.

Suggested Reading:

Secret Science Behind the Miracles, Max F. Long, 1948, $5.50, DeVorss.°

This Is Spiritualism, Maurice Barbanell, $7.50, Branden.°

°To contact these publishers directly, if you have trouble finding these books, write to: DeVorss Publishers, 1641 Lincoln Boulevard, Santa Monica, California 90404; Branden Press, 221 Columbus Avenue, Boston, Massachusetts 02116.

Chapter **32**

The Power
of Thought

A PERSON who lives a narrow life, attending to
the job at hand and devoting his spare time to mundane matters, has not reached full maturity. He goes along in his so-
called mature years, as he did in his teens or twenties. Marriage and parenthood have not wrought any great change in
him. He will reach full maturity only when he expands his consciousness.

Consciousness includes principles and conditions that are not
followed or experienced in our everyday life. Our usual acts
and thoughts concern our daily problems, and these in turn affect our being and limit our consciousness.

Think for a moment of a pebble cast into a pond or lake.
The immediate effect is on the spot where it fell, but as we
watch we see a circle of ripples spreading steadily, farther and
farther.

In the same vein, our life and problems affect not only ourselves, but also those who come in contact with us. Thus a
happy person creates happiness about him.

It follows, therefore, that we must first try to correctly assess our own situation. If it is well rounded and satisfying, we need only feel thankful and endeavor to maintain it so that we radiate happiness and, like the dropped pebble, watch our radiation or vibration have its good effect on those about us.

If, however, the weight of our problems or those of our loved ones tends to depress us we must seek and find help. Where and how?

First, we must use the Prayer of Aspiration, then follow with the Law of Assumption. In this prayer we must tell God of our wish or aspiration. At the same time, we must vividly picture our problem in our mind, but only for a very brief moment. Then, as our prayer goes on, we must call on the Law of Assumption, visualizing our problem as solved, and the results of the solution.

For example, one of our loved ones may be ill. So we must pray, asking God to restore him or her to good health. We must then picture that loved one as cured, completely well. Prayer in faith, expressed by both word and image, will bring about the desired result.

Does all this sound too hard? It is not so hard as you may think. And it is important. Let us remember that conditions of life, be they pleasant or otherwise, are largely brought about by thought. The processes of thinking constantly create the daily routine of one's life, either by perpetuating the old or producing the new.

Man gets an idea, which causes a condition to develop. For example, if health, harmony or peace is desired, it is only necessary to understand and apply the principles upon which thinking is based to achieve the desired results. Such understanding and application also provide more effective control of one's natural powers and lead to a better way of living and improvement in all conditions.

I therefore suggest that the first basic principle of thought is that mind is cause—things happen because of thoughts. The second principle is that man has the same power as his Creator, though more limited. He is a "god in the making," expressing thought and intelligence, forming ideas, understanding and manipulating the forces around and within him.

He cannot stop thinking, although he can change the nature of his thoughts. His mind-power flows through his being as does the air he breathes. He has but to direct his mind into constructive channels and give it proper expression.

From there it is but a step to the third principle: The quality of thought and its objective are important. Obviously thought should reveal a desire for perfection. Good and worthy ideas will produce good and worthy results.

The man who dedicates his life to some fine objective begins first with the idea of so doing. He not only cooperates with the greater purpose of life, but also opens himself to all the beneficent resources available to him.

Finally, the fourth principle: Thought is the highest form of energy that man uses. By it he directs and controls all other powers. So thought is power. And as we all know the world is full of products illustrating thought's creative power. For good or ill, man creates. Without the resources at his command he would achieve nothing, but his most potent forces are his thought-power and spiritual energy.

Thought is not spirit. Rather it is an expression of spirit's activity. Events and conditions are all results, external and visible effects. The invisible causes lie in the processes of thinking, of active mind-power. So, as man grows in understanding of how to recognize and use that power, his life and all he contacts must richly benefit.

How is our prayer, created by our thought, carried to the proper realm? We radiate through thinking. We send out thought waves. Experiments at Duke University and other seats of learning have proved the potency of mental telepathy. Thoughts can be sent over great distances, especially to people who are closely tied to us or those whom we love. Prayers said audibly can be helpful, but prayers sent by thought waves, in love and faith, can prove even more efficacious. We project these as a beam of light and, upon completion, acquire a feeling of fulfillment and accomplishment.

In almost the same manner, we can pray for the fruition of our heartfelt wishes and bring them to reality. A dream of a home, a marriage, children, material gain or spiritual uplift— all can be realized when our prayers are motivated by necessity, love and unselfishness. Let me illustrate:

An acquaintance of ours, a widow in her middle fifties, lived alone and held a position that did not yield abundant earnings. Her daughter was under psychiatric care, the expense of which was borne by the mother. So the lady had a problem making both ends meet and had very little to spend on clothes or personal needs. What was worse, she was not endowed with great beauty or outward charm. Small, mousy, always apologetic, she was a victim of economic deprivation and loneliness.

I saw her periodically, for business reasons, and was impressed by her utmost sincerity, her depth of religious belief and her frequent displays of kindness and goodness.

We discussed her general state and, having learned of her plight, I inquired why she had not remarried. She replied that it should be obvious why she could not even contemplate marriage. She had to wear old rags. She lacked good looks. She had a generally scrawny appearance. And she was not deluding herself into thinking she would find a willing man.

I suggested that she had inner charm, grace and goodness, and that somewhere there was a man, as lonely as herself, who would go to the end of the world to find someone like her. I then broached the Huna Method and explained the three steps to be taken, which were as follows:

> 1. After deciding that marriage to a worthy man was desirable, she was to create the man in her mind, pic-

ture him and retain the picture vividly, constantly.

2. She was to pray, in church and at her home, and with strong faith and joy see the desired event granted by God.

3. She was to buy (and did buy) a pretty nightgown, appropriately wrapped, to be put aside for the event, as a tangible expression of her faith.

After getting her to promise to do the above, I put the matter out of my mind. My experience with people has taught me not to expect humans to accept this line of thinking.

Yet within three months, I received a telephone call from her, joyfully and excitedly telling me that she had visited a friend, met a "very nice" widower from a Western state, and agreed to marry him. The couple was indeed married and the lady went West to live happily ever after.

This is an example of a principle almost 5,000 years old, but still applicable to our times. Like truth, the basic moral and religious principles live on. It is up to us to recognize God's loving kindness and bounty, to be conscious of His presence in us and about us, to reach out and realize the love and the joy of the Presence.

To summarize, in trying to solve a problem, visualize it as solved. This is the Law of Assumption. The problem visualized as healed, solved or overcome will bring the results we want.

The Huna principle applies to personal problems, business problems, and health and other problems. If it fails, it does so because somewhere, somehow, an impediment or blockage, mostly self-created, comes into play.

So remember, discipline and training are necessary and must be sustained. Deviation from the goal will result in failure.

In order to realize, to attain, to enter into effective prayer, we must enter other dimensions by attuning, through silence, to higher planes. Relaxation and peaceful surroundings are an absolute necessity. Silence, through meditation, is the ideal state. To enter into silence one must learn to meditate.

Meditation is an attempt to be a whole or integrated person. The whole person entails the physical, mental and spiritual aspects of one's self. We become a complete self when these aspects are brought into harmony. Meditation, properly performed, can bring us peace and allow us to enter into the higher realm and become one with God.

Through rhythmic breathing and worshipful attitude we attain silence and peace. At this point, we can see clouds and colors. We have truly entered a new dimension, the state of grace.

The Orthodox Jews have a blessing or benediction for almost every event of the day. They bless God upon rising in the morning, upon washing their hands before partaking of food, upon breaking bread, beginning a meal, ending a meal, going on a journey, returning from a journey, retiring, and on many other occasions, in addition to blessing Him at their regular prayer sessions, morning, afternoon and evening. All these prayers are intended to help them retain consciousness of the Presence at all times.

Although your daily program and busy life do not include such reminders, you can and should stop every once in a while and direct your thoughts and love toward the source of life and love.

Reflect on these words from an unknown author:

"Slow me down, Lord! Ease the pounding of my heart by the quieting of my mind. Steady my hurried pace with a vision of the eternal reach of time.

"Give me, amid the confusion of the day, the calmness of the everlasting hills. Break the tensions of my nerves and muscles with the soothing music of the singing streams that still live in my memory. Help me to know the magical, restoring power of sleep.

"Teach me the art of taking minute vacations for slowing down to look at a flower, to chat with a friend, to pat a dog, to answer a child's question, to read a few lines from a good book.

"Remind me each day of the fable of the hare and the tortoise, that I may know that the race is not always to the swift— that there is more to life than increasing its speed. Let me look upward into the branches of the towering oak and know that it grew slowly and well.

"Slow me down, Lord, and inspire me to send my roots deep into the soil of life's enduring values, that I may grow more surely toward the stars."

EXERCISES

MEDITATION

The proper setting for meditation is a room that lends itself to silence and excludes as much noise as possible. The sitter should use a table or desk and a straight chair. The room should be in complete darkness or lit only by a red bulb, no stronger than twenty watts.

The procedure is as follows:

1. Relax completely.

2. Utter a short prayer, acknowledging God's grace and loving kindness, and ask to be permitted to enter into grace.

3. Speak to God of your love for Him as exemplified by your love for His creation. You may whisper or speak only silently. Extend the length of your message, for it is an act of courtship of the One who loves you.

4. Begin breathing deeply, using your abdominal muscles, in the following cadence: Count eight seconds while breathing in. Count eight seconds while hold-

ing your breath. Count eight seconds while breathing out. Then repeat the process at least three times.

Once proficiency is attained, you should be in a position to see
spiritual scenes and to hear spiritual sounds or voices. You will
recognize that you have entered a state of clairvoyance and
clairaudience. For some moments you will dwell in time, instead of in space, and feel at perfect peace.

THE POWER IN WATER

1. Draw a glass of water from the tap at a temperature
   agreeable to you.

2. Take it into your silent room.

3. With your eyes closed, sip it slowly at the rate of one
   sip a second.

As the process continues, you should find a vital strength
pervading your being. Upon finishing the drink, you will feel
refreshed and uplifted.

SELF-HEALING

Since our subconscious mind manages the workings of our
physical body, it can be called upon in the event pain or discomfort overtakes us. For example, you may feel a headache
coming on. Call on your subconscious, praise it for its cooperation, and in a kindly manner request it to cure your headache.

Here, audible voice is most practical. Make your request,
then repeat several times: "My headache is leaving me. I feel
fine." After a short while, depending on how well your acquaintance or relationship has been established, your headache
will be gone.

Make sure to thank your subconscious with all due grace.

This process is applicable to most minor maladies. Care should be taken, however, to visit a doctor or dentist when common sense dictates.

THOUGHT VISUALIZATION

Go to your silent room. Offer a short prayer and ask God to grant you spiritual vision, to open your spiritual eyes.

To perform the exercise, you may stand or lie down if you wish. Usually, however, it is best to sit. Whatever your position, visualize a beam of light emanating from the area of your solar plexus. You may control this beam in any fashion you want. But in the early stages of mastering the exercise, try to visualize the beam as rising upward. After repeated practice you should be able to elongate the beam up to the ceiling. Whether you actually see the light will be indicative of how widely your spiritual eyes have been opened.

Suggested Reading:

Human Personality and Its Survival of Bodily Death,
F. W. H. Myers, out of print.°

Survival of Man, Oliver Lodge, out of print.

°Obtainable at Samuel Weiser, Inc., 734 Broadway, New York, N.Y. 10003.

Chapter 33

The Purpose of Life

OCCASIONALLY we are impelled to stop and ask ourselves: Why are we living? What is the intent and purpose of life?

Were we born to suffer? To carry a cross or burden? To endure physical sickness and mental anguish and finally to enter a cold grave?

Is life a mere matter of trial and error, chance and uncertainty?

By no means. Man is endowed with the precious attribute of free will. His whole life depends on the exercise of his free will. He becomes his own master. His way of living and thinking is his own choice.

The exercise of free will is accompanied by personal responsibility. We are responsible for our thoughts as well as our acts. We choose the type of life we live and the actions we follow. By the proper use of free will we create our own fate.

Most of us live our life in a haphazard manner, in which chance plays a major part. We are like a ship which, subject to changes in weather, may either have a tranquil journey or a storm-tossed voyage.

We must realize that our life on earth is nothing but an atelier where our character is formed and reformed, by our actions and reactions, choices and intentions, sorrows and joys, disappointments and triumphs, from the time we are born until we die. Yet it is within our own power to form our life so that we are the creator of our own fate, rather than the subject of chance.

By such exercise we also assume personal responsibility for all our acts and thoughts. If we are impelled to love mankind, to avoid doing harm or injury to our neighbor, to generally observe the Golden Rule, we put into motion and creation ideas and ideals that redound to us in like manner. But if we choose to live by chance, we become subject to all of life's vicissitudes. Our lives are not regulated by higher principles and, as the saying goes, "As you sow, so shall you reap."

Yet no choice is final. Having once made a choice, man can make another and still another as long as he wishes. He is free to will the choice. Since man is a thinker, he can choose to learn from life, to probe for purpose and meaning, until he finds an answer.

You may wonder whether our discarnate friends can help us in our economic situations, give us tips on the stock market or on horse races, or point the way to acquiring wealth in business. Perhaps our friends can help in pointing the way, but as far as I know they are bound not to do so and rarely provide information that will enrich us other than spiritually. I have been guided indirectly and up to a point. But the choice of a specific path has always been mine and thus the exercise of free will entered into the choice.

To be sure, there are cases in which we are warned about some dire event that is about to happen. Or are cautioned about our state of health or that of a relative or close friend. Or are told to do thus or so in order to overcome a condition that exists in our body. Or are aided, as often as our spiritual friends think advisable, about our state of mind.

Even so, our spiritual guides never do anything to interfere with the exercise of our free will. We must understand and clearly grasp that each person is the master of his own destiny and, as he wills it, so it comes to be.

It therefore devolves upon man to study and learn, to acquire discernment and wisdom, to learn what is good and what is bad, to gather knowledge and to lay up spiritual treasure. But how?

By developing love for mankind, thus bringing himself closer to God's loving kindness. By so doing, he will be ready at all times to give of himself and of his substance, to weigh his words so that his utterances will heal and bless, to plant a rose and uproot a thorn along life's path.

Should he ever wrong or hurt anyone, he will make amends or redress. For we hurt ourselves if we hurt others. We choose and will ourselves to do thus, for our subconscious mind contains the full record of our life, and that record is the basis of the heaven and hell we create for ourselves here and now. When we choose to live under God's law, when we choose to exercise continence and abstinence, we are rewarded with a healthy body and restful sleep. When we abide within the moral law, we are rewarded with peace of mind.

Thus the blessings or the curses of life usually result from our own choices, the workings of our free will. The record we amass is constantly under the eye of our superconscious, which makes its own entries and sheds sunlight or darkness, as the case may be.

We live for a greater purpose than mere existence. Sooner or later, we enter another sphere, bringing with us the fruits of the free will we have exercised.

We may or may not leave an imprint on history or an indelible record of achievement. As far as earthly life is concerned, we are done. It is what we take with us that counts. Our record and our aura, the notes to the song we sang.

This is our preparation for the life to come, our training ground, our school. The choices we have made, the life we have lived, will either hold us back or help us advance.

Rabbi Akiba says in the Mishna, Abot 3.16, "Everything is given on trust and the net is spread. The store is open, the shopkeeper gives on credit, but the ledger too is open, and the hand makes the entry. Whoever wishes may come and borrow, but the collectors make their daily rounds."

And so the purpose of life is to learn to live it so that it brings peace and blessings to ourselves and to others. The purpose of life is service to humanity. Our work must be directed toward this end. The products of our hands or brain should be created for this purpose.

Service to humanity is service to God. We serve the Divinity by helping the helpless, by upholding ethical standards in dealing with our fellow men, by recognizing that as we uphold, so we are upheld.

We live to serve. We live fuller lives when we serve.

Ecclesiastes, supposedly written by King Solomon, says "Vanity of vanities, all is vanity."

Yet in the *Union Prayer Book*, we read: "Our life would be altogether vanity, were it not for the soul which, fashioned in Thine image, gives us assurance of our higher destiny and imparts to our fleeting days an abiding value."

And Psalm 90 reminds us that life is short and asks God to:

Teach us to number our days,
That we may get us a heart of wisdom.

EXERCISES

MENTAL TELEPATHY
No doubt each of us has had the experience of sending a

thought to someone close to us, over a distance, and of later obtaining acknowledgment that the message was received. This process is not always intentional. We wish it and, unknowingly, the wish acts as an impulse.

But since thought is power or energy, let us learn how to send it intentionally and with worthy purpose. There are two methods.

The first actively involves both sender and receiver. Distance does not matter, but the exact time for transmitting and receiving must be prearranged. And both persons must be in a relaxed state. Strain or stress will create a block.

The sender must visualize a beam of light emanating from his solar plexus toward the receiver. The message can be spoken, but it is more effective if a silent inner voice is used.

The message should be repeated only once. The entire process should end there.

Can a conversation be carried on, in this fashion, by the two people? Yes, if both are adepts and have learned the art of true relaxation.

The second method involves no prearrangement. Indeed, the receiver does not have to be aware in advance that the message will be sent.

But both participants must be completely relaxed. In fact, the sender should transmit at a time when the receiver is asleep. If the latter is enjoying restful sleep, he will receive the message through his subconscious mind.

PSYCHOMETRY

Our spirits exude vibrations in the form of an auric substance. These vibrations create spiritual impressions on the clothes, ornaments or jewelry we wear.

As you develop spiritually and become more psychic, you should be able to psychometrize. By taking an object worn by a person, closing your eyes and lightly holding the object with the fingertips of both hands, you should receive various impressions, such as: the person's physical condition, his degree of happiness, the cause of his good or ill health and of his happiness or unhappiness, and events that have befallen him in the past.

After you have developed more fully you will be able to tell the person about his forebears, including their full names, his thoughts and aspirations, and events and conditions that will occur in his life in the future, plus much more.

This is generally referred to as a "reading." It has enriched many pseudo-mediums and brought disappointment to numerous gullible people. So it should be practiced with close relatives or old friends, until a degree of efficiency is reached, before it is attempted with strangers or casual acquaintances. Even then it should not be engaged in merely to entertain or please the curious.

Again, perfect relaxation and prayer are necessary prerequisites.

Suggested Reading:

William James on Psychical Research, Gardner Murphy, 1960, $12.50, Kelley.

Memories, Dreams and Reflections, Carl G. Jung, 1963, $10, Pantheon.

Chapter 34

Can You Be
a Medium?

AS SEEKERS after knowledge, we have begun to learn new ways, to tread new paths, to adopt new methods. Let us review briefly our purpose or program.

We began by establishing a three-fold purpose with a view to extending our knowledge beyond the usual, circumscribed limitations of everyday life. Our purpose was:

1. To investigate, become acquainted with, know our self.

2. To acquire knowledge of God, in relation to and in connection with the self.

3. To practice and apply that knowledge to our daily life and problems.

Beyond this, we set as our ultimate goal:

1. Development of our knowledge to the point where life will take on new significance.

2. Application of our minds to our bodily functions.

3. Learning the power of the spoken word.

4. Inquiry into the reason for and purpose of life.

5. Search for and attainment of the happy life.

6. Ascertainment of the means of contacting God and establishment of such contact.

We have discussed the first, second, fourth, fifth and, to some extent, the sixth points. Let us now turn to the third and, more fully, the sixth.

First, the power of the spoken word. Not many people realize fully what that power entails. Spoken words can be both a blessing and a curse. They can soothe, mollify, create beautiful pictures or carry messages of love and blessing. Spoken words of prayer, audibly recited, serve in great measure as a vehicle that impresses our subconscious, then, in turn, our superconscious. On the other hand, impulsively spoken words can wound and hurt.

Remember that whether we are silent or audible, we radiate. Spoken words strengthen this radiation and redound to ourselves. A spoken message affects the listener and the speaker. Always bear in mind that people do not respond, they react. The reaction to spoken words redounds greatly magnified and returns to the speaker, a silent but deeply felt echo, comforting or disturbing him.

Here again, the discipline of love must enter. "Think before you speak," is an old maxim. So whether you address a living person or God, always discipline your attitude and your choice of words. Even if you are angry, remember that "a kind word turneth away wrath."

Words can be weapons or ointment. Use them sparingly and wisely.

How to make contact with Eternity by ways in addition to prayer? As God is eternal, so is life eternal. Science teaches us that nothing in nature is ever wasted. The outer garments we wear, our physical bodies, are returned whence they came. Our mind, consciousness, spirit remain alive. Where, when, how?

A great number of scientists, psychologists and other people of repute have written on survival after death. Let us see what some of the best-known of them have had to say. The late Arthur Ford, internationally known medium, in his book *Nothing So Strange*, said this:

> The reach of the mind, which we call paranormal or psychic, seems to have a good deal to do with life's dimensions. We can live constricted lives, limited in our own comprehension to sensory experience, or we can learn to see through and beyond appearances. This wider comprehension is thrust upon us after death, but it lies within our power now. However, not everyone appears to be psychic. I used to ponder this fact. If the psychic faculty is so immensely useful, why is it not a common endowment? My conclusion was that it is more common than we realize and that everyone is at least potentially psychic.

William James, world-renowned psychologist, said, "The most amazing thing about psychic phenomena is their commonness. Then, certainly, the second amazing thing is their variance."

We may ask: Is everyone a potential medium? The answer is definitely yes. To what extent? It depends on the person and his own attitude and attributes. Thus some of us can learn to play the piano or sing to a proficient degree. But how many can become concert artists?

As in every other art, a great deal of time, patience and practice are required to become a medium. There are a number of steps or grades to be attained, and not everyone can attain them all.

What are the requirements?

We begin with the body and body discipline. Our eating habits must be controlled sufficiently so that our weight is kept at a proper level. This level, according to Dr. Paul Dudley White, should be the level we achieve at age twenty-two, when we reach full maturity. Our drinking habits must be watched. Water is the most important ingestant, first for its cleansing and digestive aid, secondly for its spiritual value.

Liquor should either be avoided or taken in very small amounts as seldom as possible. Hard liquor should be considered as medication. Wine, in small measure, is beneficial.

Exercise, light or vigorous according to one's needs or habit, is important. The body must be limbered up, the spine straightened, the entire physical being put in a state of flow.

Relaxation is also necessary. Breathing must be full, yet gentle. Rhythmic breathing is like a current and restores vitality.

Our minds must be rested. Otherwise, whatever our endeavor, we will be confronted by a block.

We must learn to concentrate. The student must select a very quiet place where he will be undisturbed. Conditions must be harmonious. At no time should he begin concentrating when he is disturbed or restless. The relaxing exercises discussed in the first set of exercises are most useful to establish the necessary calm. Leave your mind free of thought.

The next step is practice in imagination. Imagine a picture or a scene. Hold it and describe it to yourself in every detail. See it from every angle until it becomes a reality. Thus concentration is achieved and our minds prepared.

Our spirit or our soul is then attuned through prayer, faith and expectation. These must be sustained until you feel an at-oneness and your presence in another sphere.

Thus, psychic development progresses at three levels at the same time: body, mind, emotion. Do not try to push or you will retard your progress.

The first achievements in spiritual development are: clairvoyance, enabling one to see spiritual lights, clouds, forms and, finally, faces; psychometry, enabling one to receive impressions from intimate objects worn or carried by a person, or from notes written by a person; clairaudience, enabling one to hear the voices of spirits and to engage in automatic writing.

The next step in spiritual development is achieving the power to heal. You do not heal. But by meeting the conditions, you undergo the training that renders you suitable to be used as a healer.

In healing, intense love and complete self-abandonment are necessary. Full concentration and awareness of God's force are the key.

Further stages of development, such as the ability to lift objects, achieve trance or effect partial or complete materializations, are also attainable, mostly in the seance room.

But to achieve such steps, you are advised to engage in spiritual exercise. It consists of relaxation, meditation, and creation and maintenance of images. You will be helped. Spirits continuously seed our minds. But receptivity to this seeding depends on the individual.

Spirits act on the throat, eyes, head, down through the spine, into the pelvic region, which contains a reservoir of energy, never used physically. Spiritual force helps us to create the right conditions for further development and, if we create the right conditions, things will work for us.

If any question arises in your mind as to making a radical change in your mode of living, I definitely advise you not to do so. Unless, of course, you have been living without due consideration for others.

Thus we return to the old question: What is required of thee? The answer, of course, is, "To deal justly, to love mercy and to walk humbly with your God."

EXERCISES

THE SPOKEN WORD

Man has two methods of expression or response: the inaudible and the audible.

Inaudible responses or expressions are made through our facial features, say, through grins or grimaces. The eyes in particular reflect most vividly our inner feelings.

Audible responses include laughter, grunts, groans, sobbing and the like. They also, of course, include words, which have a great impact. A speaker can convey messages of positive or negative nature, not only by the words he speaks, but also by the volume, tone, inflection or modulation of his voice.

Having learned our lesson, we realize the importance of thinking before we speak. We must consciously bear in mind that we have expanded our spiritual horizons and, having reached this stage of advancement, must use the power of the spoken word for good.

Many of us who have household pets or birds or own horses know that our words convey a clearly understood message. Sometimes these animals are even able to read our thoughts. They do our bidding without being spoken to.

Trees and plants also react to our words. Speaking to them, with kindness and love, can advance their growth or cure their sickness.

So there is only one exercise to this lesson, to *check hasty speech and to use words wisely*, day in and day out. If you have a tape recorder, use it to record your voice. Then listen to the playback and see if you cannot get a warmer, softer note into your everyday speech.

Suggested Reading:

After Death, What? Lombroso, out of print.

Nothing So Strange, Arthur Ford and Marguerite Bro, 1971, $.75, Paperback Library.

Challenge of the Unknown, Louis Anspacher, out of print.

Many Mansions, Gina Cerminara, 1950, $6, Morrow.

The Spirits' Book, Allan Kardec, $5, The Amapse Society.°

The Guide for the Perplexed, Moses Maimonides, second edition, $5.50, Peter Smith; also available in paperback, 1904, $3.50, Dover.

They Saw Beyond (originally entitled *Witnesses for Psychic Occurrences*), 1972, paperback, $1.45, Olympia.

God's Healing Power, Edgar L. Sanford, out of print.

°Obtainable at Samuel Weiser, Inc., 734 Broadway, New York, N.Y. 10003.

Chapter 35

Practice
Makes Perfect

IN HER book *A Gift of Prophecy*, Jeane Dixon relates how someone she had befriended asked how she could repay the debt. This is how Jeane answered: "If a person helps someone and then that someone helps another, it sets up a chain of reaction. All I ever ask of you is that, if the opportunity arises and you are able, you will help someone else in need. I want no other thanks."

Those who bemoan their fate, instead of accepting life's hard bumps and pressing onward, get little sympathy from Jeane. Thoughtfully assessing the seeming inequality of man's lot, she says:

"Those with the greatest burdens may be the most blessed, if they recognize the challenge of the burdens. The richness of joy is somehow in direct proportion to the experience of suffering. Each of us has known a sense of achievement and the depth of that sense has been influenced by the failures we have known.

"Before the blooms appear so hopefully, in the spring, the

barren winter must come. If, therefore, we believe that there is a power in us which we can put to use when the need is clear, then the greater the obstacle, the greater the blessing. Call it what you will, but it brings out the best in us to overcome the obstacles of life."

In short, self-help is of utmost importance to spiritual growth. To provide yourself with the utmost help, you must learn to relax, to achieve mental balance, to acquaint yourself with your subconscious and arrive at a working arrangement with it, to pray and commune.

To some people, however, these lessons are just so much rhetoric. They will not take the time to practice the exercises. They will not walk to the tap to quench their thirst. They would prefer it if someone brought them the drink, while they loll in their usual state of inactivity. These are the physically or mentally torpid.

Many bear their self-imposed cross like a halo. It gives them a feeling of martyrdom, and woe to any and all who would deprive them thereof.

Other people have no control over their subconscious. Indeed, the subconscious has, over the course of time, become their master and, despite its own low mental power and inability to reason, has subdued the conscious part of the mind and become ruler of the roost.

The results are obvious to all except the person involved. He or she has lost a sense of propriety in eating, drinking, dressing and general appearance. He or she has passed the point at which they should have stopped and considered how they look to someone else.

Thus if you are to grow spiritually, it is important that you first clean up physically, morally and spiritually. It is also important that you not approach the exercises I have included in the immediately preceding chapters haphazardly. They require constant practice and repetition. You must apply yourself to them earnestly and steadily. Otherwise nothing will happen.

Each set of exercises should be practiced separately, one at a time, until they are mastered, before you proceed to the next step. The process cannot and must not be rushed.

It is comparable to planting flowers. The soil must be prepared, the seed planted, the garden watered and weeded before the flowers will bloom.

It is all up to you. You will take out what you put in.

One final thought: In seeking to enrich your spiritual life, keep three principles in mind. Take everything with a grain of salt. Keep a sense of humor. Exercise a healthy amount of skepticism.

All is possible so long as you keep your feet on the ground.

Chapter 36

The Challenge of Our Times

FOR YEARS, the Western world, and America in particular, has poured economic and other material aid into underdeveloped countries. Has it all been enough? Are we giving the very best that is in us?

Some people do not think so. A few years ago, Dr. Charles Malik, former president of the United Nations General Assembly and later professor of philosophy at the American University in Beirut, Lebanon, desperately urged the West to give spiritual and human aid as well. And yet he wondered if we were spiritually enough developed to provide it. In a speech to an international congress on management, he said:

> When will the West in its contact with the rest of the world recover dimension of spirit, depth and character —a dimension inherent in it more wonderfully and more originally than in any other civilization in the world?
>
> They are all technicians whom it produces . . . A

168

world of perfect technicians is . . . a dreary and boring world, where there is nothing beyond man and his mastery over nature, including his mastery over other technicians through his scientific management of them.

Perfect hierarchy, perfect organization, total efficiency; but no spirit, no freedom, no joy, no humor, and therefore no man.

Technique, efficiency, management, results! But what does the poor man in these countries live for? Is he free to think and seek the truth? Nay, tell us, is there a truth to seek, and is freedom therefore at all important?

Form, form, form; technique, technique, technique. Nobody asks the fundamental question as to what is the whole blooming thing for? Nobody cares to find what spirit pervades the whole thing. Nobody has the time to ascertain whether man in his freedom and fullness exists at all.

Roads, dams, efficiency and the smile of the rulers— that is all that matters; but spirit, freedom, joy, happiness, truth, man—that never enters the mind. . . .

I want no man to be hungry or ignorant or diseased, but the question is· What will people live for once they are not hungry, once they are no longer ignorant, and once they suffer from no disease whatever?

Do you want to create a civilization in which Socrates, Plato, Augustine and Aquinas, Pascal and Kant will feel completely out of place? If you do not, then you must tell us, what are your ends, what are your ideals, what is the quality of values you wish your children to seek and love and realize, what is the spirit and soul that animates your whole civilization, what do you believe in, what do you really stand for, whom do you worship and whom do you want your children to worship?

Scientific and technological advances are occurring at a pace that almost overwhelms us. Changes have been swift and far-reaching. Travel, communications, electronics, medicine have all developed to an unprecedented degree. As the pace of social change is also accelerating, standards and institutions that have remained unchanged for centuries are breaking down.

The rapidly increasing world population creates a menacing problem. The world political situation is seething.

Industrialization has produced an urban society and weakened some of the stabilizing forces that used to keep things in balance. In a predominantly agricultural society, the family kept its members together, enforced acceptable behavior, and instilled a sense of security. But today there is widespread evidence that old family ties are breaking asunder.

Religion used to impress us in a power greater than our own. It added significance to life and taught us that death does not mean the extinction of personality. It made us confident that virtue and suffering were rewarded and wickedness punished in the world to come. People governed their lives accordingly.

Today, however, there is a weakening of religious faith. Old dogmas are held in doubt. Scientific advances have helped increase skepticism of religious symbols and rituals. Ministers, rabbis and priests are all struggling with the problem with little success. Bible reading is almost extinct. There is vagueness and lack of conviction.

Relaxation of family discipline and religious conviction has cast many individuals on their own resources. The results often are mental illness, alcoholism, drug addiction, juvenile delinquency, crime, divorce, and general demoralization.

Our hearts and souls seem to be adrift. We feel a lack, a great void. There is a spiritual hunger abroad. Many have turned to other religions, to Ethical Culture, to Zen Buddhism, to the various sciences for an answer without realizing heartfelt satisfaction. The pursuit of happiness continues. But the goal is elusive.

The world is full of pride and prejudice, bitterness and disappointment, frustration, sickness and hunger.

And yet many of us have almost been lulled to sleep. Big cities and their commercial enterprises tend to channel our thinking process to the point where we consider any small minority that does not conform as odd or "way out."

We spend our time keeping up with the Joneses or a step ahead of them. We conform in our way of living, dressing, thinking and talking. We are part of a herd.

What is the answer?

The past had given us a legacy of truth and wisdom. We must reinterpret it in the light of modern times. The earnest seeker, willing to learn and discover, can be shown the way.

Man has been endowed with attributes of the mind that make it possible to reach for and acquire the knowledge necessary to his well-being, his wholeness. Instead of being small and circumscribed, his horizons can be enlarged if his mind will only reach forth.

There is no real mystery in the world, except the mystery that exists within man himself. The theory of spiritual consciousness removes the mystery, for it reveals that man has infinite mental energy, as infinite as that of electricity or any other natural energy. Although we cannot see this energy, we can observe the results of its use.

Science has begun to recognize and explore the reality of the spiritual realm most of us cannot see, hear or touch. At the same time various attempts have been made to reconcile scientific discovery and religion. Much serious thinking has been given to ways of closing the breach between the two.

But how are we to consider religion? What is true religion? Is it theology as promulgated by the various religious creeds? Is the whole truth contained in the philosophies of the Jewish, Protestant, Roman Catholic, or Hindu teachings?

Spiritualism points to a belief that is universal. It removes all barriers. It lifts man's thinking to a higher plane, where he embraces his fellow man instead of separating himself from him.

By acknowledging everlasting life and learning of God's love for all His creatures, man transcends most of his limitations. He enters into the spiritual spheres, where he needs no palatial edifice, no ritual, no incantation. His home becomes his temple, his altar, his refuge, his oasis in a strife-torn world.

By learning to use his mind to a fuller extent and by sincere, programmed exercise of his mind, man enters into a state of oneness with the abiding God-spirit, a state where all problems can be solved, and where peace, happiness and contentment can be realized in full measure.

INDEX